N.c. ΕΡ

The politics of B

1688–1800

D0611913

The eighteenth century was a complex period in British political history. This new study provides an up-to-date and comprehensive analysis of both the structures of eighteenth-century politics – national and local – and the major issues that provided the dynamic of a period that was far from static. The author considers the situation not only in England, but also in Ireland, Scotland and Wales.

The central emphasis of the book is on the interrelationship of political structure and content. Jeremy Black argues that power was not solely sought for its own sake, but also in order to advance or sustain particular policies and interests. He also stresses that this was true not only of Whitehall, Westminster and royal palaces centring around London, but also of parish vestries, town councils and commissions of the peace throughout the country.

This study provides the ideal introductory textbook for students. In addition to its lucid analysis, it acquaints students with the most recent historiographical developments in the subject and the text is supported by a section of documents, most of which have not been printed before.

Jeremy Black is Reader in History at the University of Durham.

NEW FRONTIERS IN HISTORY

series editors

Mark Greengrass
Department of History, Sheffield University

John Stevenson
Worcester College, Oxford

This important new series reflects the substantial expansion that has occurred in the scope of history syllabuses. As new subject areas have emerged and syllabuses have come to focus more upon methods of historical enquiry and knowledge of source materials, a growing need has arisen for correspondingly broad-ranging textbooks.

New Frontiers in History provides up-to-date overviews of key topics in British, European and world history, together with accompanying source material and appendices. Authors focus upon subjects where revisionist work is being undertaken, providing a fresh viewpoint which will be welcomed by students and sixth-formers. The series also explores established topics which have attracted much conflicting analysis and require a synthesis of the state of the debate.

Already published

C. J. Bartlett Defence and diplomacy: Britain and the great powers, 1815–1914

Forthcoming titles

Paul Bookbinder The Weimar Republic

Joanna Bourke Production and reproduction: working women in Britain, 1860–1960

Michael Braddick The nerves of state: taxation and the financing of the English state, 1558–1714

Ciaran Brady The unplanned conquest: social changes and political conflict in sixteenth-century Ireland

David Brooks The age of upheaval: Edwardian politics, 1899–1914

David Carlton Churchill and the Soviets

Carl Chinn Poverty and the urban poor in the nineteenth century

Barry Coward The Cromwellian Protectorate

Conan Fischer The rise of the Nazis

Neville Kirk The rise of Labour, 1850–1920

Tony Kushner The holocaust and its aftermath

Keith Laybourn The General Strike of 1926

Alan O'Day Irish home rule

Panikos Panayi Immigrants, minorities and British society, 1815–1919

Daniel Szechi The Jacobites: Britain and Europe, 1688–1788

John Whittman Fascist Italy

The politics of Britain
1688–1800

Jeremy Black

Manchester University Press
Manchester and New York
Distributed exclusively in the USA and Canada by St. Martin's Press

Copyright © Jeremy Black 1993

Published by Manchester University Press
Oxford Road, Manchester M13 9PL, UK
and Room 400, 175 Fifth Avenue, New York, NY 10010, USA

Distributed exclusively in the USA and Canada by
St. Martin's Press, Inc., 175 Fifth Avenue, New York, NY 10010, USA

British Library Cataloguing-in-Publication Data
A catalogue record for this book is available from the British Library

Library of Congress Cataloging-in-Publication Data
Black, Jeremy.
  The politics of Britain, 1688–1800 / Jeremy Black.
    p. cm. — (New Frontiers in History)
  Includes bibliographical references and index.
  ISBN 0-7190-3760-3 (hardback). — ISBN 0-7190-3761-1 (pbk.)
  1. Great Britain—Politics and government—18th century. 2. Great
  Britain—Politics and government—1869–1702 3. Great Britain
  Politics and government—Revolution of 1688. I. Title.
  II. Series.
  DA480.B56 1994
  820.941—dc20   93–10228
                                                                  CIP

ISBN 0 7190 3760 3 *hardback*
ISBN 0 7190 3761 1 *paperback*

Printed in Great Britain
by Bell and Bain Ltd, Glasgow

Contents

Preface and acknowledgements

In a necessarily brief treatment of a huge subject, only certain themes can be highlighted. The choice, in particular the emphasis on tensions within society and the political system, reflects both my detailed research on a number of aspects of the period, and my experience of teaching the subject for a number of years. I would like to thank fellow scholars with whom I have discussed the subject as well as the students I have taught at Durham for obliging me to clarify my views. I would like to thank the British Academy and the Staff Travel and Research Fund of Durham University for supporting the archival research on which this book is based. I owe a particular debt to John Stevenson for asking me to undertake this volume, to him, Peter Borsay, Eveline Cruickshanks, John Derry, Grayson Ditchfield, David Eastwood, William Gibson, Richard Harding, Colin Haydon, Nicholas Henshall, Brian Hill and Peter Luff for commenting on earlier drafts, and to Wendy Duery for all her help. Studying the period has always been for me a source of pleasure and I hope I can communicate some of the excitement and insights that it offers.

Newcastle, December 1992

Abbreviations

Add.   Additional Manuscripts
BL.   London, British Library, Department of Manuscripts
Bod.   Oxford, Bodleian Library
fo.   folio
HMC.   Historical Manuscripts Commission
PRO.   London, Public Record Office
SP.   State Papers
RO.   Record Office

Unless otherwise stated, all works are published in London.

For Ian Christie and Andrew McHallam

Introduction

In the 1980s, historians writing about British politics in the eighteenth century primarily addressed the question of the nature of society in that period. An alternative approach that would stress the autonomy of politics, its essential independence from wider social developments, and would focus on details of political alignment and manoeuvre, has received less attention. Instead, debate has centred on the stability, or otherwise, of British society, the forces for change and order, the relationship, adversarial or symbiotic, of change and continuity. It is in this context that politics has primarily been considered and political activity has generally been seen as an expression of this wider social politics.[1]

Yet it has also been clear that such an approach, the use of models stressing change, continuity, or, less commonly but more profitably, both, has its limitations. As in other aspects of organised human activity, in this – and other – periods, for example religion, law and order, education and social welfare, it is necessary to note that the role of more general trends was accompanied by, and in many respects mediated through, more specific processes. These reflected, in large part, particular practices and attitudes and the nature of distinct institutional cultures. In the political sphere this implies that it is necessary to recognise the autonomy of Parliament, electoral processes, and the 'political thought' of the period, while also accepting that they were part of a wider political world and aspects of the social system.

Another limitation is that of scale. Most work on eighteenth-century politics has been on the national scale. This suffers from two problems. First, there is a tendency to treat Scotland,[2] Ireland[3] and England in isolation; Wales is a special case, as it lacked any institutional basis for political identity and had been integrated effectively into the institutional and representative structure of the English realm by Henry VIII.[4] If the British dimension is to be meaningful, it is necessary to consider Scotland, Ireland and England/Wales, not simply in terms of their own development and specialist schools of historians, but also with reference to their interrelationships.[5] Second, it is probable that a stress on the national scale underrates both the importance and autonomy of local politics, and the diversity of the local dimension of national politics. This is true not only of England, but of the other parts of Britain as well.

One of the most striking features of British historiography is that the stress on the vitality and importance of the regional aspect of politics, on the county community, in the sixteenth and seventeenth centuries, and indeed in the medieval period as well, has not been matched in work on subsequent periods. There are of course significant exceptions,[6] but, nevertheless, it is still reasonable to say that we know all too little about the local and regional dimensions of eighteenth-century politics. This has several serious consequences. It means that undue weight has been placed on those local political worlds that have been studied. These have been largely major cities, above all London, but also Bristol, Exeter, Newcastle and Norwich,[7] and, as a result, are atypical and may display a level and type (the two are related but different) of politicisation that provides little guide to the situation in smaller towns and rural areas. Secondly, in so far as there has been scholarly study, attention has been concentrated on the local dimensions of particularly spectacular national political campaigns, such as the opposition to the Excise bill in 1733, the Wilkite agitation of the 1760s, or criticism of the confrontation with the American colonists in the mid-1770s.[8]

Again, this stress on the atypical may reveal not the essential characteristics of the general situation, but an unusual set of circumstances when local and national alignments were interrelated and symbiotic to an exceptional degree. The local and regional dimensions of eighteenth-century British politics have to be rescued from a habit of assuming that they were material only when national issues were being agitated, and freed from a teleology that sees the development of a national political consciousness, or at least national political parties, as the end result, necessary end and only topic of consequence.

This misleading impression is related to another, the emphasis on crisis and crises. Crisis, division and conflict are often seen as central features of British political history, not least because of a somewhat misleading view that change, which is what fascinates most historians, is their product. As a result, British history is often taught as a sequence of crises, in the case of medieval English history attention being focused on the Norman Conquest, Magna Charta, Simon de Montfort etc. In this perspective the English/British civil wars seem the most important episode of the early modern period, and the eighteenth century is most of interest for the development of radicalism and the question of how revolution was avoided in the period 1780–1820. Thus, one of the most influential books of the 1970s, John Brewer's study of the 1760s, concluded with a hackneyed image that summed up the sense of inexorable change towards public politics: '. . . the tide of popular politics rising, even after it had fluctuated to a low ebb . . . made the parliamentary politicians look ever more like the ill-fated King Canute'.[9] This interpretation is linked to a chronology of increasing stability in the late seventeenth and early eighteenth centuries, culminating in the oligarchical Whig regime of the age of Walpole[10] and Pelham, followed by growing tension, radicalism and instability.

Recent studies have made the descriptive accuracy of this chronological framework appear increasingly invalid, and have thus called into question the related explanatory model. Instead, it is now clear not only that a different chronology can be offered, but also that the nature of political crisis in the eighteenth-century context has to be re-examined.[11] This is related to the last change in emphasis that has to be outlined in an introduction because it is crucial to the nature of politics in this period as in others: the role and nature of issues. If the structure and chronology of politics are to be understood, it is necessary also to focus on the content. This does not involve denying the importance of the pursuit of office and the nature of patronage, both crucial components of traditional studies of eighteenth-century politics, but rather explaining that power was sought not only for its own sake but also in order to advance or sustain particular policies and interests; and that this was true not only of Whitehall, Westminster and the royal palaces in and around London, but also of parish vestries, town councils and commissions of the peace throughout the country. Indeed, it has been argued that power was sought in order to advance particular world views framed by religious values.[12] In a short work it is only possible to elaborate some of these themes, but the central emphasis in what follows is on the interrelationship of structure and content, the issues that provided the dynamic of a period that was far from static.

Notes

1 Influential works include J. Brewer, *Party Ideology and Popular Politics at the Accession of George III* (Cambridge, 1976); J. Cannon ed., *The Whig Ascendancy* (1981); J. C. D. Clark, *English Society 1688–1832: Ideology, social structure and political practice during the ancien regime* (Cambridge, 1985); L. Colley, *In Defiance of Oligarchy: the Tory Party 1714–60* (Cambridge, 1982); H. T. Dickinson, *Liberty and Property: political ideology in eighteenth-century Britain* (1977); P. Langford, *A Polite and Commercial People: England 1727–1783* (Oxford, 1989).

2 Valuable introductory works include R. Mitchison, *Lordship to Patronage: Scotland, 1603–1745* (1983); J. S. Shaw, *The Management of Scottish Society, 1708–64* (Edinburgh, 1983).

3 T. W. Moody and W. E. Vaughan eds., *Eighteenth-Century Ireland 1691–1800* (Oxford, 1986).

4 P. Jenkins, *The Making of a Ruling Class: the Glamorgan gentry, 1640–1790* (Cambridge, 1983); T. Herbert and G. E. Jones eds., *The Remaking of Wales in the Eighteenth Century* (Cardiff, 1988).

5 D. Szechi, 'The Hanoverians and Scotland', in M. Greengrass ed., *Conquest and Coalescence: the shaping of the state in early modern Europe* (1991), pp. 116–33; Colley, *Britons: forging the nation 1707–1837* (New Haven, 1992).

6 J. Money, *Experience and Identity: Birmingham and the West Midlands 1760–1800* (Manchester, 1977); W. A. Speck, 'Northumberland elections in the eighteenth century', *Northern History*, XXVIII (1992), pp. 164–77; P. D. G. Thomas, 'The rise of Plas Newydd: Sir Nicholas Bayly and county elections in Anglesey, 1734–84', *Welsh History Review*, XVI (1992), pp. 160–76. Sheffield is presented as 'largely free of political strife', in D. Hey, *The Fiery Blades of Hallamshire: Sheffield and its neighbourhood, 1660–1740* (Leicester, 1992), pp. 293–9. The crucial role of personalities in a more far-flung and generally ignored region is read-

ily apparent from R. P. Fereday, *Orkney Feuds and the '45* (Kirkwall, 1980) and *The Orkney Balfours 1747–99* (Oxford, 1990). For criticism of too great a stress on the county dimension, A. Hughes, *Politics, Society and Civil War in Warwickshire, 1620–1660* (Cambridge, 1987).

7   J. Stevenson ed., *London in the Age of Reform* (Oxford, 1977); G. S. DeKrey, *A Fractured Society: the politics of London in the first age of party, 1688–1715* (Oxford, 1985); N. Rogers, *Whigs and Cities: popular politics in the age of Walpole and Pitt* (Oxford, 1989); R. Newton, *Eighteenth Century Exeter* (Exeter, 1984).

8   For example T. R. Knox, 'Popular politics and provincial radicalism: Newcastle-upon-Tyne, 1769–1785', *Albion*, XI (1979), pp. 220–39, and 'Wilkism and the Newcastle election of 1774', *Durham University Journal*, LXXII (1979–80), pp. 23–37;'"Bowes and Liberty": The Newcastle by-election of 1777', *Durham University Journal*, LXXVII (1985), pp. 149–64; J. E. Bradley, *Popular Politics and the American Revolution in England: petitions, the Crown, and public opinion* (Macon, Georgia, 1986) and *Religion, Revolution and English Radicalism. Non-conformity in eighteenth-century politics and society* (Cambridge, 1990).

9   Brewer, *Party Ideology*, p. 269.

10   J. H. Plumb, *The Growth of Political Stability in England 1675–1725* (1967).

11   J. Black, *Robert Walpole and the Nature of Politics in Early Eighteenth Century England* (1990), pp. 101–5.

12   Clark, *English Society*.

1

Eighteenth-century Britain

Eighteenth-century Britain really began in 1688. The 'Glorious Revolution' of that year led to constitutional change, set a new political agenda and transformed the relationship between the constituent political parts of the British Isles. It was to be the central point of reference in subsequent discussion of the political system and played a crucial role in the public ideology of the state for over a century. And yet the events of that year have to be understood not only in terms of their future significance, but also as a consequence of the divisions, tensions and fears of seventeenth-century British politics, especially those of the 1670s and 1680s.

In 1688 the last male Stuart ruler of Britain, James II, was driven from the throne by William of Orange, William III.[1] This, the last successful political coup d'état or revolution in British history, reflected hostility to the policies and Catholic faith of James, king from 1685 to 1688. There was a long-standing suspicion that the Catholics would try to seize power by conspiratorial means. This might appear foolish to modern eyes, but Protestants could look back to the conspiracies against Elizabeth I in favour of the Catholic Mary Queen of Scots, as well as to the Gunpowder Plot against James I in 1605. Paranoid tension rose to a peak with hysteria about a Popish Plot in 1678. This led to the Exclusion Crisis (1678–81), an attempt to use Parliament to exclude James from the succession and to weaken the government of his elder brother, Charles II (king 1660–85), who lacked any legitimate children. Exclusion's leading advocate, Anthony,

Earl of Shaftesbury, created what has been seen as the first English political party, the 'Whigs', an abusive term referring to Scottish Presbyterian rebels, originally used by their opponents. The Whigs produced a mass of propaganda. The first unlicensed newspaper made clear its didactic nature in its title, *The Weekly Pacquet of Advice from Rome . . . in the process of which, the Papists arguments are answered, their fallacies detected, their cruelties registered, their treasons and seditious principles observed . . .*

Anti-Catholicism could help create a crisis, but the Whigs suffered from the determination of most people to avoid both rebellion and a repetition of the chaos of the Civil Wars of the 1640s; the strength of Charles's position in the House of Lords and the king's right to summon and dissolve Parliament as he thought fit, both of which blocked Exclusion in a legal fashion; the lack of a generally agreed alternative to James; and Charles's fixed determination. With Scotland and Ireland securely under control, Charles II did not face a crisis comparable to that which had undermined his father, Charles I, in 1638–41, and he avoided foolish moves such as his father's attempt to arrest the Five Members.

Whig failure was followed by a royalist reaction that was eased by Charles's negotiation in 1681 of a subsidy from Louis XIV of France, which enabled him to do without Parliament for the rest of his reign. Louis was not only the most powerful monarch in western Europe, but also a Catholic ruler noted for his actions against his Protestant minority. Whig office holders were purged and Whig leaders fled or were compromised in the Rye House Plot (1683), an alleged conspiracy to assassinate Charles and James. This led to executions and stimulated an attack on Whig strongholds. Corporation charters, most notably that of London, were remodelled in order to increase Crown influence, and Dissenters (Protestant non-Anglicans, many of whom were Whigs) were persecuted with increased severity. Thus, the Exclusion Crisis had polarised politics. In some respects there was a return to the divisions, tensions and anxieties of the 1650s after an easing of tension in the 1660s. This polarisation was to persist and to have a major effect on the politics of the reigns of William III and Anne.

Thanks to the reaction against the Exclusion Crisis, James II was able to succeed his brother with little difficulty (1685). His political situation was strengthened that year by the defeat of rebellions in Scotland and England. Charles II's most charismatic bastard, James, Duke of Monmouth, had pressed a claim to be Charles's heir during the Exclusion Crisis, arguing that Charles had really married his mother, Lucy Walter. In 1685 Monmouth sought to overthrow James. He landed at Lyme Regis on 11 June 1685 and won widespread support in Dorset and Somerset. At Sedgemoor, on the night of 5/6 July, Monmouth nearly succeeded in a surprise attack on the royal army. His force was, however, routed with heavy casualties. Monmouth was executed and some of his supporters transported to the colonies or hanged after biased trials in the 'Bloody Assizes' of Chief Justice George Jeffreys.

Like Oliver Cromwell, victory gave James a conviction of divine approval, and the rebellion led him to increase his army, but Parliament was unhappy about this and especially with the appointment of Catholic officers. James prorogued Parliament in November 1685, and, with less constraint, moved towards the catholicising of the government. This was to make him unpopular. The changes necessary to establish full religious and civil equality for Catholics entailed a destruction of the privileges of the Church of England, a policy of appointing Catholics, the insistent use of prerogative action, and preparations for a packed Parliament. James took steps to develop the army into a professional institution answerable only to the king.[2] And yet, despite the concern created by royal policies and the Protestant association of Catholicism with arbitrary government, there was no revolution in Britain. Unlike the situation in 1638–42, the Stuart monarchy was now strong enough to survive domestic challenges, and there was no breakdown of order in Scotland and Ireland.

The birth of a Prince of Wales on 10 June 1688 was a major shock to those disgruntled with James's politics. 'It could not have been more public if he had been born in Charing Cross', noted Francis Atterbury, but unhappy critics spread the rumour that a baby had been smuggled into the Queen's bed in a warming pan. Hitherto, James had had no surviving children from his fifteen–year Catholic second marriage, but had two daughters, Mary and Anne, living from his Protestant first marriage. Mary was married to James's nephew, William III of Orange, who was the leading Dutch political figure, a Protestant and the most active opponent of Louis XIV. A Catholic son threatened to make James's changes permanent. Nineteen days after the birth, Archbishop Sancroft of Canterbury and six bishops were acquitted on charges of sedition for protesting against James's order that the Declaration of Indulgence granting all Christians full equality of religious practice, a move that challenged the position of the Church, be read from all pulpits. There is still controversy as to whether James advanced a policy of toleration as a matter of religious principle, or as a move of political expediency designed to win the support of Protestant nonconformists for an assault on the position of the Church of England that would largely benefit Catholics.

The more volatile and threatening situation led seven politicians to invite William to intervene in order to protect Protestantism and traditional liberties. Motivated rather by a wish to keep Britain out of Louis XIV's camp, William had already decided to invade. In many respects his invasion was a gamble, dependent on whether Louis XIV decided to attack the Dutch, on the policies of other powers, the winds in the North Sea and Channel, and the response of the English fleet and army. After his initial invasion plan had been thwarted by storms, William landed at Torbay on 5 November 1688. He benefited from a collapse of will on the part of James, who had an army twice the size of William's. James had been a brave naval commander earlier in his life, but in 1688 he suffered from a series of debilitating nosebleeds and a collapse of will, and failed to lead his army into battle. As James's resolve failed, the morale of his army disintegrated, and a vacuum of power developed. Most people did not want any breach in the hereditary succession, and William had initially pretended that he had no designs on the Crown. However, as the situation developed favourably, especially when James had been driven into exile, William made it clear that he sought the throne. This was achieved by declaring it vacant and inviting William and Mary to occupy it as joint monarchs. By claiming that it was only a vacancy that was being filled it was possible to minimise the element of innovation.[3] All Catholics were debarred from the succession: a resolution was passed that 'it hath been found by experience to be inconsistent with the safety and welfare of this Protestant kingdom to be governed by a Popish prince'. The anti-Catholic atmosphere of the period was reflected in such publications as *London's Flames Revived . . . By all which it appears, that the said fires were contrived, and carried on by the Papists* (1689). Past episodes, such as the Great Fire of London (1666), could thus be revived and integrated into a coherent account of the nation's situation past and present. That the monarchy was hereafter to be Protestant was one of the central results of 1688–9.

What was to become known as the Glorious Revolution was both the last successful invasion of England and a coup in which the monarch was replaced by his nephew and son-in-law, albeit one that also benefited from significant domestic support. It also led in 1689 to war with Louis XIV, who gave James II shelter and support, and the need for parliamentary backing for the expensive struggle with the leading power in western Europe helped to give substance to the notion of parliamentary monarchy. The financial settlement of 1689 left William with an ordinary revenue that was too small for his needs, but, anyway, the outbreak of war obliged William to meet Parliament every year. The Triennial Act (1694) ensured regular meetings of Parliament, and, by limiting their life span to three years, required regular elections. William's was truly a constricted monarchy. The Dublin Parliament also became a regular and central feature of the Irish constitution after the Glorious Revolution, sitting every second year from 1692.[4]

The Glorious Revolution was to play a crucial role in the English public myth, to be celebrated as such at the 1988 tercentenary, to be seen as the triumph of the liberal and tolerant spirit, the creation of a political world fit for Englishmen. This interpretation never made much sense from the Scottish or Irish perspective and it has recently been seriously challenged. What was for long seen as an irresistible manifestation of a general aspiration by British society for progress and liberty can now be seen, as it was by contemporaries, as a violent rupture, an ideological, political and diplomatic crisis. The cost of William's invasion was not only a civil war that brought much suffering to Scotland and Ireland, but also a foreign war that, as well as shaping the nature of the Revolution Settlement, created considerable stresses within Britain.

James II was resolved to regain his throne and the Glorious

Revolution thus launched Jacobitism, as the cause of the exiled Stuarts came to be known from the Latin for James, Jacobus.[5] Initially, James controlled most of Ireland and had support in Scotland. This situation looked back to the last period of Stuart dispossession, the English Civil Wars and Interregnum. However, William III, like Cromwell in 1649–53, was to succeed in having the Stuarts and their supporters driven from Scotland and Ireland, thus forcing them to become reliant on foreign support that was offered in accordance with a diplomatic and military agenda, timetable and constraints that rarely suited the Jacobites.

James's position in Scotland collapsed in December 1688. The Convention of the Estates which met in Edinburgh the following March was dominated by supporters of William and on 4 April 1689 the crown of Scotland was declared forfeit, William and Mary being proclaimed joint sovereigns a week later. Catholics were excluded from the Scottish throne and from public office. The contractual nature of the Revolution Settlement, the extent to which the Crown had been obtained by William and Mary on conditions, was far more apparent in Scotland than in England. James's standard was raised in Scotland in April 1689 by John Graham of Claverhouse who was backed by the Episcopalians, the supporters of a Scottish Church controlled, like that of England, by bishops. At the battle of Killiecrankie on 27 July, Claverhouse's Highlanders routed their opponents with the cold steel and rush of a highland charge, but their leader was killed and the cause collapsed under his mediocre successors. Most of the Highland chiefs swore allegiance to William in late 1691.[6]

James II's supporters dominated most of Ireland in 1689 though Derry, fearing Catholic massacre, resisted a siege and was relieved by the English fleet. James landed in Ireland in March 1689 with a small French force. In 1690 William, who had crossed to Ireland with an army including Danish, Dutch and German contingents, outflanked the outnumbered James at the battle of the Boyne on 1 July and captured Dublin. The following year brought further success for the Williamite cause, including victory at Aughrim. By the Treaty of Limerick (1691), the Jacobites in Ireland surrendered, many, the 'Wild Geese', going to serve James in France.[7]

Ireland was then subjected to a Protestant ascendancy. The

11

Catholics had held 59 per cent of the land in 1641 and 22 per cent in 1688. By 1703 this had fallen to 14 per cent, by 1778 to 5 per cent. Catholic officials and landowners were replaced and parliamentary legislation against Catholics was passed. Catholics were prevented from freely acquiring or bequeathing land or property and were disfranchised and debarred from all political, military and legal offices and from Parliament. By legislation of 1704 property inherited by Catholics was, unless they converted, to be transferred to their nearest Protestant relatives. Bishops and regular clergy were banished, parish priests compelled to renounce loyalty to the Stuarts. Acts forbade mixed marriages, Catholic schools and the bearing of arms by Catholics. The culture of power in Ireland became thoroughly and often aggressively Protestant, so that, even when in 1749 the Dublin election was contested by Protestant zealots, the charge of popery and Jacobitism appeared the most effective that could be used against rivals. The Catholic percentage of the population did not diminish, however, because serious repression was episodic and indeed difficult given the inadequate coercive machinery available to the government; while the Catholic clergy, wearing secular dress and secretly celebrating mass, continued their work, sustained by a strong oral culture, the emotional link with a sense of national identity, by hedge-school teaching and by a certain amount of tacit government acceptance. The Church hierarchy survived largely intact.[8]

The Glorious Revolution led to English domination of the British Isles, albeit domination that was helped by and shared with important sections of the Irish and Scottish population, Irish Anglicans and, more significantly, Scottish Presbyterians. The alternative had been glimpsed in 1689 when James II's Parliament in Dublin had rejected much of the authority of the Westminster Parliament. This path had, however, been blocked. Jacobitism, and the strategic threat to England, posed by an autonomous or independent Scotland and Ireland, pushed together those politicians in the three kingdoms who were in favour of the Revolution Settlement. The Union of 1707 between England and Scotland arose essentially from English concern about the possible hazards posed by an autonomous, if not independent, Scotland, and from Scottish economic weakness. There was some support for the measure in Scotland, though its passage through the Scottish Parliament ultimately depended on corruption, self-interest and determination not to be shut out from the English and colonial market. The Union gave Scotland forty-five MPs in the Westminster House of Commons and sixteen peers, elected by an assembly of Scottish peers, in the House of Lords; an under-representation of Scotland's population, but an over-representation of her economic strength. The terms were negotiated in 1706 and ratified by the Scottish Parliament on 16 January 1707. That Parliament came to an end as a result of the Union. In 1708 the new Parliament of Great Britain abolished the Scottish Privy Council, the principal executive agency for Scotland, and thus ensured that there would be one British Privy Council sitting in London. From 1708 for most of the period until 1725, and then again in 1742–6 there was a separate Scottish Secretary of State, but, thereafter, Scottish affairs were not the responsibility of a separate Secretary of State until Gladstone reintroduced a Scottish Secretaryship.[9]

In the early eighteenth century there was support for Union with England in Ireland, too: the Irish Parliament petitioned for it in 1703 while Union had been considered by English ministers in 1697. It seemed, however, to have little to offer to English politicians, and Ireland was treated with scant consideration. The Westminster Parliament's Declaratory Act of 1720 stated its supremacy over that of Dublin. Legislation in Westminster, the result of protectionist lobbying by English interests, for example the Irish Woollen Export Prohibition Act of 1699, hindered Irish exports, while the granting of Irish lands and pensions to favoured courtiers accentuated the problem of absentee landowners and revenue-holders, with a consequent loss of money to the country. A sense of exploitation was exacerbated by particular steps. In 1722 a Wolverhampton ironmaster, William Wood, purchased a patent to mint copper coins for Ireland, a step that led to bitter complaints in Ireland, where constitutional and political weakness were seen as leading to economic problems. Walpole's government was obliged as a result of the agitation to recall the patent, and, thereafter, greater care was taken of Irish sensitivities, though the relationship with England was still far from equal. The Irish Parliament had to pay the cost of quartering a large part of the army in Ireland to support the Anglo-Irish establishment and, from the English point of view, to hide the size of the army from English public opinion. Long-standing religious grievances helped to exacerbate Irish political disaffection in the 1790s. Indeed, the French Revolution served in Ireland as a catalyst to activate long-standing politico-religious tensions.[10]

England might dominate Britain clearly after 1691, but, for the politically involved groups at least, a sense of separate identity and national privileges continued to be important in Ireland and Scotland, though not Wales. This sense of separation was accentuated at the ecclesiastical level, as in 1689 the Scottish Parliament abolished Episcopacy and in 1690 a Presbyterian Church was established there. As a result, the Union of 1707 led to the creation of a multi-confessional state. Though possibly over 80, or even 90, per cent of its population used Welsh as the medium of communication, Wales, however, lacked centralising institutions, or social, ecclesiastial and legal arrangements corresponding with its linguistic distinctiveness.[11] Ireland retained its Parliament until the Act of Union of 1800 and the need to manage this Parliament obliged British politicians to turn to Irish 'undertakers'. This was not, however, an easy process, as they 'could never be certain who in Ireland could be trusted with political power or for how long, what would satisfy, or what would work'. The preservation of a Parliament in Dublin enabled Ireland's Protestant politicians to retain a measure of importance and independence, so that British ministers faced difficulties in devising strategies for managing the Parliament and governing Ireland. Scotland had a different national Church, and legal system, from England. And yet, the sense of separate identity was weakened, especially at the level of the élite, by the decline of Celtic languages and the growing appeal of English cultural norms and customs.[12]

Welsh, Irish and Scots sought to benefit from links with England. Scots came to play a major role in the expansion of empire, not least through service in the army. This process had begun in the seventeenth century, especially under William III (William II of Scotland). On the eve of the parliamentary union, Scots held 10 per cent of the regimental colonelcies in the British army and between 1714 and 1763 this increased to 20 per cent. James Murray, brother of a prominent Jacobite, followed a distinguished military career that led to his becoming a full general and, successively, Governor of Quebec, Canada, Minorca and Hull. Lord John Murray, who also had prominent Jacobite relations, died the senior general in the army. Some of the Irish aristocracy, such as Marquess Wellesley and his younger brother, the Duke of Wellington, devoted themselves to British politics and service to the empire as a whole. Edmund Burke's parents were both born Catholics, but his father's conversion to Anglicanism and his own upbringing in the same faith enabled Burke to pursue a political career in England. Protestantism, war with France and the benefits of empire helped to create a British nationhood, which developed alongside the still strong senses of English, Scottish and Irish identity.[13]

The nature of British society in the period has been a matter of some controversy. It is possible to discern aspects or intimations of the modern world, to see a rising middle class and an age of Reason, a polite and commercial people, aristocratic ease and elegance, urban bustle and balance, a land of stately homes and urban squares, Castle Howard, Blenheim, Bath, the West End of London, Georgian Dublin, and the New Town of Edinburgh. Brick buildings with large windows were built in a regular 'classical' style along and around new boulevards, squares and circles. Parks, theatres, assembly rooms, subscription libraries, race-courses and other leisure facilities were opened in many towns. The total stock of public buildings in the West Riding of Yorkshire rose from about ninety in 1700 to over five hundred by 1840.[14]

Different images and views can, however, be advanced. Élite cultural achievement was matched by relatively few changes in the 'life-style' or expectations of the majority of the population. Serious disease played a major role in what was a hostile environment. The plague epidemic of 1665–6, which killed over 70,000, was the last in England: mutations in the rat and flea population were more important in preventing a repetition than clumsy and erratic public health measures and alterations in human habitat thanks to construction with brick, stone and tile. There were still, however, other major killers, including a whole host of illnesses and accidents that can generally be tackled successfully in modern Europe. Measles epidemics killed many young children in, for example, 1705–6, 1716 and 1718–19. In the last, child burials accounted for 61 per cent of total deaths in

Bewdley. A high rate of child mortality there in 1676 may have been due to infant diarrhoea. Smallpox, typhus, typhoid and influenza were serious problems. The year could be divided by the prevalence of different diseases: smallpox in spring and summer, dysentery in spring and autumn. In late 1750 over a hundred people were recorded as having died in Kidderminster of 'malignant sore throat with ulcers'.[15] Primitive sanitation and poor nutrition exacerbated the situation. The limited nature of the housing stock led to the sharing of beds, which was partly responsible for the high incidence of respiratory infections. Problems of food shortage and cost ensured that the bulk of the population lacked a balanced diet even when they had enough food.

Illiteracy was widespread, more pronounced among women than men, and in rural than in urban areas. Illiteracy in rural Dorset in the 1790s was 56 per cent of newly-weds.[16] Such levels necessarily limited the numbers who could actively follow the public politics made possible by the tremendous expansion of the press from the lapsing of the Licensing Act in 1695. The burgeoning chap-book market, however, suggests that this was a society where reading was also pretty widespread.[17] By the mid-century most adults were probably able to make out a printed notice. The sheer volume of such material, whether ephemera or more substantial pieces of local administrative material, such as the militia lists of 1757 or calls for recruits, suggests that there was a public for such items even if it was less prevalent in more rural areas.

William Hogarth (1697–1764) caricatured in his paintings the vigorous, if not seamy, side of life in London, the centre of political activity and consciousness, a thriving metropolis where organised crime, prostitution and squalor were ever-present, venereal disease and destitution much feared. The criminal code, which has been seen as a means to control political and social dissidence,[18] decreed the death penalty, or transportation to virtual slave labour in British colonies, for minor crimes; the game laws laid down harsh penalties for poaching and permitted the use of spring guns by landlords.[19] Under the Transportation Act of 1718, passed in order to deal with the rise of crime in perfunctorily-policed London, 50,000 convicts were sent to America by 1775 for seven or fourteen years or life; the loss of America (1775–83) was followed by consideration of transportation to

Africa and, finally, in 1788, the establishment of a convict settlement in Australia. A feeling of crisis and insecurity indicates that, in so far as there was an aristocratic and establishment cultural and political hegemony, it was in part bred from élite fear, rather than from any sense of confidence or complacency. Continuity was sought for, not because of any easy complacency, but rather as a result of the realisation of social fragility. Aristocratic portraits and stately homes arguably reflected a need to assert tradition and superiority and to project images of confidence against any potential challenge to the position of the élite. There were bitter political and religious disputes in eighteenth-century Britain. The succession was a cause of division and instability until the crushing of Bonnie Prince Charlie, eldest son of the Jacobite claimant to the throne, at Culloden in 1746. The disestablishment of Episcopalianism in Scotland after the Glorious Revolution, and the sense of 'The Church in Danger' from Dissenters and Whigs in England, fed tension. Though William III (1689–1702) and, to a greater extent, George I (1714–27) and George II (1727–60), relied heavily on the Whigs, the continued existence of a popular and active Tory party was a challenge to the practice of Whig oligarchy,[20] as was the existence of vigorous traditions of urban political activity.[21]

The supposed politeness of early eighteenth-century Augustan literature does not survive an attentive reading of Alexander Pope or Jonathan Swift, much of whose work is spiked with bitterness and sometimes savage satire. A stately vocabulary was used to express violent attitudes. The impulse for order which has been seen as a dominant motif of the age, displayed and expressed in the architecture and literature of the period, should not be regarded as a simple reflection of some political and social reality. Rather, the commentators, writers and artists of the period stressed the need for order because they were profoundly aware of the threats to that order around them. Likewise, it is important to stress the continued importance of religion, both in itself and in other spheres of life. Religious concerns still constrained and influenced the content of much cultural activity. This was a volatile and varied cultural world in which politics and religion were far from placid, and in which much that might seem irrational was far from marginalised. Far from being a cool Age of Reason, it saw the religious enthusiasm that led to the foundation of Methodism,[22] as well as the huge market for almanacs. Millenarian and providential notions were not restricted to a minority. Isaac Newton (1642–1727), from 1703 President of the Royal Society, a body established in 1660 to encourage scientific research, discovered calculus, universal gravitation and the laws of motion, but also searched for the date of the Second Coming. Newton argued that God acted in order to keep heavenly bodies in their place. Science was not therefore to be incompatible with the divine scheme. There was a widespread interest in alchemy. The eminent chemist Peter Woulfe (c. 1727–1803), who developed an apparatus for passing gases through liquids, also pursued alchemical investigations, fixing prayers to his apparatus. Superstition was commonplace.

There was also a profound sense of disquiet about the very nature of society, coming not so much from radicals as from clergy, doctors and writers concerned about moral and ethical values.[23] Morality was a crucial cultural motif, and one that was fundamental to political debate and language (discourse): civic and personal honour, corruption and consistency were central themes. Hogarth's moral satires were a considerable success. The engravings of his series *The Harlot's Progress* sold over a thousand sets and were much imitated. The plays of Colley Cibber, George Colman, George Lillo and Oliver Goldsmith propounded a secular morality opposed to vice and indulgence. The etiquette of the period condemned dishevelment and slovenliness in clothing. Samuel Richardson's *Pamela* (1740), the first of the sentimental novels, was a very popular work on the prudence of virtue and the virtue of prudence. These works provided the cultural context within which politicians were judged publicly. They were expected to behave like noble Romans, to aim at exemplary conduct, not the calculations of power and patronage. Few contemporaries were as convinced as later historians that theirs was an age of stability. For them stability in culture and politics was perhaps regarded as something which had existed in the past and was now increasingly lost, or as something which should be worked towards; it was hardly something which had been achieved and which still existed: unless through constant vigilance.

The extent to which British politics should be seen as distinctive is a central question, and one that requires a consideration of wider similarities or contrasts. There were obvious differences between British society and societies on the Continent. These included the demographic and economic prominence of the capital, London, and the high percentage of the labour force not engaged in agriculture. There was less of a distinction, political, social and legal, between town and countryside than in much of the Continent. Merchants and financiers, mostly from London, were able to acquire rural estates and to become local political patrons. Common legal rights and penalties were more likely to exist in Britain than in most Continental states, a point underlined by contemporaries when Earl Ferrers was hanged for murder in 1760. The rotation of crops and use of legumes that increasingly characterised East Anglian agriculture, and the growing use of coal, were not mirrored across most of Europe. Urban mercantile interests were more politically significant than in other large European states. One of the principal reasons for divergence between England and the Continent was the relative sophistication of England's primary financial institutions, especially the Bank of England, established in 1694.

And yet, it would be inappropriate to focus on such differences and to suggest that therefore it is unhelpful to consider Britain in a European context. 'Progressive' features of British agriculture and industry were matched elsewhere. The agricultural techniques of East Anglia owed much to those of the province of Holland, while coal was already used for industrial processes in a number of Continental regions, such as the Ruhr and the Pays de Liège. If many miles of canals were constructed in Britain in the eighteenth century, the same was true of Russia. Industrial development was not restricted to Britain, but also existed in a number of Continental regions, such as Bohemia and Silesia.

Once the basic similarity of technological aspects has been appreciated, the economic picture is not, however, one of searching for comparisons or contrasts between Britain and the Continent, for Britain is unhelpful as a unit for analysis. The variations between, and indeed within, regions within Britain were such that it is more pertinent, as in more recent times, to note common indicators between individual British and Continental regions rather than to stress the divide of the Channel. There was no nation state as far as economic experience and trajectory were concerned. Though national in their scope, the protectionist and regulatory legislation enacted by British (and Continental) governments did not create effective economic spaces.

In socio-economic terms, it is, therefore, possible to stress similarity, as well as contrast, between Britain and the Continent. This is more problematic as far as politico-constitutional aspects are concerned. The 'Glorious Revolution' led to a contemporary emphasis on specificity that has been of considerable importance since. The Whig tradition made much of the redefinition of parliamentary monarchy in which Parliament met every year, of regular elections, the freedom of the press, protection from arbitrary arrest, religious toleration, and the establishment of a funded national debt guaranteed by Parliament (Doc. 1). The Revolution Settlement, the term applied to the constitutional and political changes of the period 1688–1701, was seen by its supporters as clearly separating Britain from the general pattern of Continental development. Indeed, to use a modern term, it was, for them, as if history had ended, for if history was an account of the process by which the constitution was established and defended, then the Revolution Settlement could be presented as a definitive constitutional settlement, and it could be argued that the Glorious Revolution had saved Britain from the general European move towards absolutism and, to a certain extent, Catholicism. In 1689, and again during the celebrations of the Glorious Revolution in 1789, it was asserted that the right of resistance was a unique, never to be repeated event, and that it applied only to James II. The Jacobite challenge meant, however, that this achievement was seen as under threat. In Strasburg in 1753 Voltaire, the leading, and certainly most fashionable, European intellectual, who had spent 1726–8 in London, told William Lee, a well-connected English tourist, that he came from 'the only nation where the least shadow of liberty remains in Europe'. For fashionable intellectuals on the Continent, Britain offered a model of a progressive society,[24] one that replaced the Dutch model that had been so attractive the previous century, though there was also criticism of aspects of British society. Many eighteenth- and nineteenth-century French and German historians and lawyers looked to Britain (by which they tended to mean England) as culturally and constitutionally superior, and thus as a model to be copied. With time, Britain became more important as an economic model and a source of technological innovation that attracted industrial espionage.[25]

Many foreign commentators, however, underrated the divisions in eighteenth-century British society. Politics, religion, culture and morality, none of them really separable, were occasions and sources of strife and polemic, and the same was true not only of views of recent history, most obviously the Revolution Settlement, but also of the very question of the relationship between Britain and the Continent. Alongside the notion of uniqueness as derived from and encapsulated in that Settlement, there was also a habit, especially marked in opposition circles, of seeking parallels abroad. Thus, the long ministry of Sweden's Count Horn could be compared with that of Walpole, while *Fog's Weekly Journal*, the leading Tory paper, could suggest in 1732 that the Parlement of Paris was readier to display independence than the Westminster Parliament; a total reversal of the customary Whig view. This habit was accentuated from 1714 by the Hanoverian connection, for under both George I and George II the contentiousness of that connection led to a sustained political discourse about the extent to which Britain was both being ruled in accordance with the foreign interests of her monarchs and being affected in other ways, especially cultural.

Britain was not the only European maritime and trans-oceanic imperial power, though her naval strength and colonial possessions had grown considerably since the mid seventeenth century. Hers was the politics of a growing imperial power. The legislation of the Westminster Parliament affected more and more of the world. Indeed, there were complaints about the growing influence of oceanic mercantile interests in Parliament, specifically of 'nabobs', men who had made their fortunes trading with India and returned to buy up pocket boroughs (seats where the representation was effectively controlled). Such complaints, however, neglected the role of Parliament in commercial and imperial legislation. Britain's control of the eastern seaboard of North America north of Florida had been expanded and consolidated with the gain of New York from the Dutch (1664), the French recognition of Nova Scotia, Newfoundland and Hudson's Bay as British (1713), and the foundation of colonies including Maryland (1634), Pennsylvania (1681), Carolina (1663) and Georgia (1732). Possibly 200,000 people emigrated from the British Isles to North America during the seventeenth century, far outnumbering the French settlers in Canada and Louisiana, and the settlements founded included Charleston (1672), Philadelphia (1682), Baltimore (1729) and Savannah (1733). The English also made a major impact in the West Indies, acquiring Bermuda (1609), St Kitts (1624), Barbados (1625), Antigua and Montserrat (1632) and Jamaica (1655) and developing a sugar economy based on slave labour brought from West Africa, where British settlements included Accra (1672). The East India Company, chartered in 1600, was the basis of British commercial activity, and later political power, in the Indian Ocean. Bombay was gained in 1661, Calcutta in 1698.

Trade outside Europe became increasingly important to the British economy, and played a major role in the growth of such ports as Bristol, Glasgow, Liverpool and Whitehaven. The mercantile marine grew from 280,000 tonnes in 1695 to 609,000 in 1760,[26] the greater number of experienced sailors providing a pool from which the navy could be manned, in part by the dreaded press gangs. Co-operation between the financial circles of the City of London and the landed interest was crucial to the economy, to public finance and to the imperial expansion of Britain. Parliament's role in imperial regulation became far more marked from the 1760s, with lengthy and contentious discussion of the financial contribution to be made by the colonies especially the Stamp Act Crisis (1765–6), debate over the government of Quebec (1774) and serious division over the government of British India and the relation between the East India Company and the government (1766, 1773, 1783–4). Nevertheless, despite the importance of finance, trade and empire, there was, as on much of the Continent, a hostility to new wealth, to urban enterprise and capitalism.[27]

The Glorious Revolution is crucial to the Whig myth, or interpretation, of British history, central to the notion of British uniqueness. This concept can, however, be queried by comparing Britain and the Continent in the post-1688 period in both a functional and an ideological light. Functionally, the crucial relationship in both was that of central government and aristocracy, a term that in Britain, from an operative viewpoint, should be taken to include the more substantial landed gentry. The aristocracy owned and controlled much of the land and were the local notables, enjoying social prestige and effective governmental control of the localities (Doc. 2). They dominated the parliamentary system, Church, central and local government and the armed forces. The position of the aristocracy was supported by intellectuals, educational institutions and widely-diffused social attitudes. Both Anglicanism and classical, patrician ideals endorsed an aristocratic social order. Aristocratic influence strengthened in many spheres during the eighteenth century, though the élite were divided over politics rather than united in furtherance of social interests. Alongside, however, the obvious role of the social élite, it is also clear that the governing group included men of property at all levels, that the national and local dimension of public life depended on and incorporated less prestigious wealthy propertied members of the the community.[28]

Central government meant in practice, in most countries, the monarch and a small group of advisers and officials. The notion that they were capable of creating the basis of a modern state is misleading. Central government, itself a questionable term because of its modern connotations and its suggestions of bureaucratic organisation, lacked the mechanisms to intervene effectively and consistently in the localities. In addition, in what was, in very large part, a pre-statistical age, the central government of any large area lacked the ability to produce coherent plans for domestic policies based on the premiss of change and development. Without reliable, or often any, information concerning population, revenues, economic activity or land ownership, and lacking land surveys and reliable and detailed maps, governments operated in what was, by modern standards, an information void. The contrast with the established Churches of the period is instructive. Thanks to their possessing a universal local system of government and activity, the parochial structure, and an experienced and comprehensive supervisory mechanism through their hierarchies, the Churches were able to operate far more effectively than secular government, not least in collecting information. The first British census was not until 1801, while no large-scale cadastral mapping survey was carried out in Britain until the Tithe Commutation Act of 1836 when payments in kind were replaced by monetary rents.

Lacking the reach of modern governments, those of early modern Europe relied on other bodies and individuals to fulfil many functions that are now discharged by central government, and they reflected the interests, ideology and personnel of the social élite. Whatever the rhetoric and nature of authority, the reality of power was decentralised and, therefore, consensual, though the terms of the consensus varied. Social welfare, health and education were largely the responsibility of ecclesiastical institutions or of lay bodies, often with religious connections, such as the Society for Promoting Christian Knowledge, which encouraged the foundation of charity schools in the early eighteenth century. The Dublin and Westminster parliaments both took steps in these fields, but they were largely a product of lobbying by interest groups and certainly did not match the universal state regulation that was to be introduced the following century.[29] Education in England had to be paid for by the pupil's family, which was generally the case in the grammar schools, or by a benefactor, dead or alive.[30] The regulation of urban commerce and manufacturing was largely left to town governments. The colonels of regiments were often responsible for raising their men, and, in part, for supplying them also, as the administrative pretensions of the early modern state in military matters were generally unrealised, especially in so far as land forces were concerned,[31] though the British navy was administratively, as well as militarily, impressive.[32] Most crucially, the administration of the localities, especially the maintenance of law and order and the administration of justice, was commonly left to the local aristocracy, whatever the formal mechanisms and institutions of their authority. In so far as such matters can be seen in terms of power relationships,[33] and thus of a politics that encompassed the whole of society, it is clear that the fundamental configuration of power and politics was inegalitarian, hierarchical, male-dominated, heritable, and reverential and referential to the past; and that this did not alter during the century.

In all these respects, Britain can be seen as yet another Continental state, for, despite the constitutional differences, the shared reality at the local level was self-government of the localities by their notables and at the national a political system that was largely run by the aristocracy. Visually and politically, the countryside was dominated by aristocratic seats, and this not only remained the case throughout the period, but became more pronounced. Sir John Vanbrugh (1664–1726), the exponent of the

English baroque, displayed at Blenheim, Castle Howard and Seaton Delaval a degree of spatial enterprise similar to the architects of princely palaces on the Continent. Robert Adam (1728–92) rebuilt or redesigned many stately homes, including Harewood House, Kedleston Hall, Kenwood, Luton Hoo and Syon House, his work redolent with classical themes. Landscape gardening, inescapably linked to wealthy landed patronage, flourished and was influential abroad. The architect William Kent (1684–1748) developed and decorated parks (grounds of houses) in order to provide an appropriate setting for buildings. Lancelot 'Capability' Brown (1716–83) rejected the rigid formality associated with Continental models, contriving a setting that appeared natural, but was nevertheless carefully designed for effect, a suitable motif of the life-style of the political élite. Brown's landscapes of serpentine lakes, gentle hills and scattered groups of newly-planted trees swiftly established a fashion, in a world where the small number of patrons and their interest in new artistic developments permitted new fashions to spread swiftly, while their wealth enabled them to realise and develop these fashions. Brown's ideas were developed further by Humphry Repton (1752–1818), in accordance with the concept of the 'Picturesque', which stressed the individual character of each landscape and the need to retain it, while making improvements to remove what were judged blemishes and obstructions and to open up vistas, this treatment of nature symbolising the general values of society. Landscape gardening and decoration were of direct interest to some members of the élite, to Richard, 1st Viscount Cobham at Stowe, and to his protégé, William Pitt the Elder, who helped to lay out the grounds of his friends' seats, and erected a temple dedicated to Pan and a garden pyramid at South Lodge, Enfield. Pride of possession characterised Pitt, who became 1st Earl of Chatham, like other landlords. He had a public way which crossed his Somerset estate of Burton Pynsent sunk between deep hedges in order to hide it from view.[34]

The key to stable government in Britain, as on the Continent, was to ensure that the local notables governed in accordance with the wishes of the centre, but this was largely achieved by giving them the instructions that they wanted. For the notables it was essential both that they received such instructions and that they got a fair share of governmental patronage. This system worked and its cohesion, if not harmony, was maintained, not so much by formal bureaucratic mechanism, as by the patronage and clientage networks that linked local notables to nobles wielding national influence and enjoying access to the monarch. This was very much the case in Britain. The strength and vitality of the British aristocracy in the post-1688 world is readily apparent, not least because there was no sharp divide between the peerage and the wealthy commoners, mostly landed, who, in large part, dominated and comprised the House of Commons. The extent to which central government agencies and pressure could be important in the localities has recently been emphasised, but, nevertheless, at the local level, the gentry, as Justices of the Peace, were the dominant figures. They had been entrusted with much of the business of government in the localities from the fourteenth century, and their role continued whoever directed affairs in London. Law and order depended on the JPs.[35] In Hanoverian Britain the gentry were also, as commissioners, the crucial figures in the local allocation of the Land Tax.[36] The Lords Lieutenant of Counties, usually prominent aristocrats, and, in seaboard counties, the Vice Admirals, also played a major role in government. One of the latter, Sir Jonathan Trelawny, Bishop of Exeter 1689–1707, organised preparations against a possible French invasion of Devon in 1691.[37]

The system cohered through patronage and personal connection, leaving copious documentation in the private correspondence of prominent politicians, such as Thomas, Duke of Newcastle, Secretary of State 1724–54, and First Lord of the Treasury, 1754–6, 1757–62.[38] Patronage and connection could, however, lead to, or foster, division among the élite. The Lords Lieutenants and Deputy Lieutenants of counties, for example, were chosen as a result of political affiliation, and not simply social status, and they were expected to ensure that their counties were politically responsive to the views of the government. In some areas there were constant feuds between local grandees. In Cardiganshire, for example, the vicious and unpopular Sir Herbert Lloyd, MP 1761–8, had serious disputes with Wilmot, 1st Earl of Lisburne, the Pryses of Gogerddan and the Powells of Nanteos on issues such as control of the Surveyorship of Royal Mines in Wales and the arranging of local elections. In 1755 Lloyd was dismissed as a JP for abusing his position. The bitter mid-century electoral history of the county was essentially a matter of personal and family divisions.[39] Ideology played little role there in the 1750s. In Anglesey the Whig challenge to Tory hegemony between 1689 and 1730 was an aspect of the challenge by local squires to the dominant Bulkeley family, and was exacerbated by the personal rivalry of Richard, 4th Viscount Bulkeley and Owen Meyrick MP.[40]

The central role of the Crown and royal Court was another aspect of political life that Britain shared with most Continental states. In place of earlier notions about the impotence of Anne and, particularly, the first two Georges, most scholars now emphasise their political importance.[41] The royal Court was a social and political centre in which politicians spent much time. The monarch's powers remained considerable. This was especially true in foreign policy[42] and army patronage. Ministers were appointed by and answerable to the monarch. With the exception of George III during his attacks of porphyria, all the monarchs of the period were capable of fulfilling the obligations of their office: there were no minors and thus no regency governments comparable to that of Louis XV in 1715–23. William III's successors in Britain lacked his intellectual ability, but were, nevertheless, monarchs of shrewdness and some political skill.

Aside from the 'functional' similarity between Britain and the Continent, the crucial relationship of government and élite, there was also an 'ideological' counterpart in the form of a shared belief in the rule of law and of government being subject to it. The constitutional mechanisms by which this should pertain varied in Europe, but there was a common opposition to despotism.

Thus, the public myth of uniqueness that played such a major role in the Whig inheritance (by the 1770s all politicians could see themselves as Whigs), can be qualified, and indeed was by domestic critics who charged, with reason, that, once in office, the Whigs had abandoned their late seventeenth-century radical ideas, and who denied that the British system was different from and better than other systems across the Channel. Particular attention was focused on the way in which the 'executive' had allegedly subverted the freedom of Parliament by corruption. What was in fact being criticised was the search for, and in some respects, re-creation of stable government by means of a new consensus. In this consensus, patronage and the avoidance of radical changes were dominant, and thus the path of government was smoothed by practices that lessened the chance of unpredictable developments, practices that neutered political activity in short. Therefore, despite the role of a permanent and quite effective Parliament, the Old Corps (ministerial) Whigs could be seen as having created during the reigns of George I and George II a state that bore comparison both with strong Continental monarchies and with that attempted by the Stuarts, and such comparisons were to be pressed home both then and in the 1760s and early 1770s when George III broke with the tutelage of the Old Corps Whigs and allegedly sought to create a stronger monarchy. Contemporaries searched for parallels in the Maupeou Revolution in France (1771) and in Gustavus III's coup in Sweden (1772), both seen as measures designed to subordinate 'intermediate institutions' to Crown authority, and in the Swedish case a coup d'état for the monarchy. Many British politicians made comparisons between Britain and Sweden after 1772 to the latter's disadvantage. The apparent degree of difference between Britain and the Continent was also eroded by the widespread process of public politicisation on the Continent. In France that led to and, to a greater extent, was stimulated first by the mid-century controversies centring on Jansenism and later by those arising from the Maupeou Revolution.

It would be mistaken to exaggerate the placidity and predictability of eighteenth-century British politics. An excellent recent account of popular agitation, especially collective violence, in Ireland has argued that although England and Scotland saw unrest, riots and agitation, there was nothing to compare with the 'lower class secret societies' of Ireland 'engaged in sustained, systematic campaigns of violence and intimidation'. Earl Fitzwilliam's contrasting of violent Meath and his home country of Northamptonshire in 1795 has been cited, and yet a recent account of Northampton's politics in 1795–6 concluded that 'beneath this tranquil surface lay passions which . . . burned with an intensity which the modern mind may find hard to comprehend'. The nature and context of political activity were very different, but the bitterness of partisanship was shared.[43] The theme of an 'irrational' intensity of commitment was one that was voiced by contemporaries. In 1702 the prominent Tory politician, Henry St John, later Viscount Bolingbroke, wrote 'Men are generally governed by humour and seldom by reason. They scarce ever make use of their own eyes, but party, caprice, nay lust and passion, are so many false optics through which they look at everything.'[44]

Notes

1   Speck, *Reluctant Revolutionaries: Englishmen and the revolution of 1688* (Oxford, 1988); E. Cruickshanks ed., *By Force or By Default? the revolution of 1688–1689* (Edinburgh, 1989); G. H. Jones, *Convergent Forces: immediate causes of the Revolution of 1688 in England* (Ames, Iowa, 1990); R. Beddard ed., *The Revolutions of 1688* (Oxford, 1991); J. I. Israel ed., *The Anglo-Dutch Moment: essays on the Glorious Revolution and its world impact* (Cambridge, 1991); L. G. Schwoerer ed., *The Revolution of 1688–1689* (Cambridge, 1992).

2   J. Miller, *James II* (1978); J. Childs, *The Army, James II, and the Glorious Revolution* (Manchester, 1980).

3   Miller, 'Crown, Parliament, and people', in J. R. Jones ed., *Liberty Secured? Britain before and after 1688* (Stanford, 1992), pp. 78–9.

4   P. G. M. Dickson, *The Financial Revolution in England* (1967); D. W. Jones, *War and Economy in the Age of William III and Marlborough* (Oxford, 1988).

5   B. Lenman, *The Jacobite Risings in Britain 1689–1746* (1980); Cruickshanks ed., *Ideology and Conspiracy: aspects of Jacobitism 1689–1759* (Edinburgh, 1982); Cruickshanks and Black eds., *The Jacobite Challenge* (Edinburgh, 1988); Black, *Culloden and the '45* (Stroud, 1990).

6   P. Hopkins, *Glencoe and the End of the Highland War* (Edinburgh, 1986); I. Cowan, 'The reluctant revolutionaries: Scotland in 1688', in Cruickshanks ed., *By Force*, pp. 65–81, and 'Church and state reformed? the Revolution of 1688–9 in Scotland', in Israel ed., *Anglo-Dutch Moment*, pp. 163–84; A. M. Scott, *Bonnie Dundee, John Graham of Claverhouse* (Edinburgh, 1989).

7   J. G. Simms, *Jacobite Ireland 1685–1691* (1969); W. Troost, *William III and the Treaty of Limerick* (Leiden, 1983); P. Wauchope, *Patrick Sarsfield and the Williamite War* (Blackrock, 1992).

8   S. Murphy, 'Charles Lucas and the Dublin election of 1748–1749', *Parliamentary History*, II (1983), p. 101; Simms, *The Williamite Confiscation in Ireland, 1690–1703* (1956); M. Wall, *The Penal Laws, 1690–1760* (Dundalk, 1961); L. M. Cullen, 'Catholics under the penal laws', *Eighteenth-Century Ireland*, I (1986), pp. 23–36; T. P. Power and K. Whelan eds., *Endurance and Emergence: Catholics in Ireland in the eighteenth century* (Dublin, 1990).

9 P. Riley, *The English Ministers and Scotland 1707–1727* (1964) and *The Union of England and Scotland* (Manchester, 1978); C. A. Whatley, 'Economic causes and consequences of the Union of 1707: a survey', *Scottish Historical Review*, LXVIII (1989), pp. 150–81.

10 A. Goodwin, 'Wood's halfpence', *English Historical Review*, LI (1936), pp. 647–74; S. J. Connolly, *Religion, Law, and Power: the making of Protestant Ireland 1660–1760* (Oxford, 1992); J. Smyth, *The Men of No Property: Irish radicals and popular politics in the late eighteenth century* (1992), pp. 10, 32.

11 P. Jenkins, *A History of Modern Wales 1536–1990* (Harlow, 1992), pp. 2–3.

12 R. E. Burns, *Irish Parliamentary Politics in the Eighteenth Century: I, 1730–60* (Washington DC, 1991), p. 337; Jenkins, *Glamorgan Gentry*, pp. 239–73.

13 J. Hayes, 'Scottish officers in the British army, 1714–63', *Scottish Historical Review* XXXVIII (1958), pp. 385–7; A. Murdoch, *The People Above: politics and administration in mid-eighteenth century Scotland* (Edinburgh, 1980), pp. 132–3; K. M. Brown, 'From Scottish Lords to British Officers: state building, élite integration and the army in the seventeenth century', in N. MacDougall ed., *Scotland and War AD 79–1918* (Edinburgh, 1991), p. 149; Colley, *Britons*.

14 P. Borsay, *The English Urban Renaissance: Culture and Society in the Provincial Town, 1660–1770* (Oxford, 1989); Langford, *Polite and Commercial People*; K. Grady, *The Georgian Public Buildings of Leeds and the West Riding* (Leeds, 1989).

15 Bewdley Historical Research Group, *Bewdley in its Golden Age: life in Bewdley 1660–1760* (Bewdley, 1991), pp. 35, 43; J. Landers, *Death and the Metropolis* (Cambridge, 1993).

16 G. J. Davies, 'Literacy in Dorset, 1750–1800', *Notes and Queries for Somerset and Dorset*, vol. XXXIII part 333 (March 1991), pp. 24–5.

17 Black, *The English Press in the Eighteenth Century* (1987); V. Neuburg, *Popular Education in Eighteenth Century England* (1971) and *The Penny Histories* (1965).

18 D. Hay, P. Linebaugh and E. P. Thompson, *Albion's Fatal Tree* (1975), but also see J. H. Langbein, 'Albion's fatal flaws', *Past and Present*, XCVIII (1983), pp. 96–120; P. King, 'Decision-makers and decision-making in the English criminal law, 1750–1800', *Historical Journal*, XXVII (1986), pp. 25–58; J. Innes and J. Styles, 'The crime wave in recent writing on crime and criminal law', *Journal of British Studies*, XXV (1986), pp. 380–435; R. B. Shoemaker, *Prosecution and Punishment: Petty Crime and the Law in London and Rural Middlesex c. 1660–1725* (Cambridge, 1991).

19 P. B. Munsche, *Gentlemen and Poachers: the English game laws, 1671–1830* (Cambridge, 1981).

20 Colley, *In Defiance of Oligarchy*; P. K. Monod, *Jacobitism and the English People 1688–1788* (Cambridge, 1989).

21 Rogers, *Whigs and Cities*.

22 R. E. Davies and E. G. Rupp, *A History of the Methodist Church in Great Britain I* (1965); A. Armstrong, *The Church of England, the Methodists and Society, 1700–1850* (1973).

23 Black and J. Gregory eds., *Culture, Politics and Society in Britain 1660–1800* (Manchester, 1991).

24 G. Bonno, *La Constitution britannique devant l'opinion française de Montesquieu à Bonaparte* (Paris, 1931); J. Grieder, *Anglomania in France 1740–1789: fact, fiction and political discourse* (Geneva, 1985); Black, 'Meeting Voltaire', *Yale University Library Gazette*, LXVI (April 1992), pp. 167–9.

25 J. R. Harris, *Essays in Industry and Technology in the Eighteenth Century: England and France* (Aldershot, 1992), pp. 18–175.

26 R. Davis, *The Rise of the English Shipping Industry in the Seventeenth and Eighteenth Centuries* (1962); W. Minchinton ed., *The Growth of English Overseas Trade in the Seventeenth and Eighteenth Centuries* (1969); K. Morgan, *Bristol and the Atlantic Trade in the Eighteenth Century* (Cambridge, 1993).

27 P. J. Cain and A. G. Hopkins, 'The political economy of British expansion overseas, 1750–1914', *Economic History Review*, XXXIII (1980), p. 469, and 'Gentlemanly capitalism and British expansion overseas', *Economic History Review*, XXXIX (1986), pp. 503–14; P. Lawson, *The Imperial Challenge: Quebec and Britain in the age of the American Revolution* (Montreal, 1989); L. S. Sutherland, *The East India Company in Eighteenth Century Politics* (Oxford, 1952); H. Bowen, *Revenue and Reform: the Indian problem in British politics 1757–1773* (Cambridge, 1991); J. Raven, *Judging New Wealth: popular publishing and responses to commerce in England 1750–1800* (Oxford, 1992).

28 Cannon, *Aristocratic Century: the peerage of eighteenth-century England* (Cambridge, 1984); Langford, *Public Life and the Propertied Englishman 1689–1798* (Oxford, 1991).

29 W. L. Parry-Jones, *The Trade in Lunacy: a study of private madhouses in England in the eighteenth and nineteenth centuries* (1972); J. Woodward, *To Do the Sick No Harm: a study of the British voluntary hospital system to 1875* (1974); T. Laqueur, *Religion and Respectability: Sunday Schools and working-class culture* (New Haven, 1976); R. K. McClure, *Coram's Children: the London Foundling Hospital in the eighteenth century* (New Haven, 1981).

30 R. S. Tompson, *Classics or Charity? the dilemma of the eighteenth-century grammar school* (Manchester, 1971).

31 A. J. Guy, *Oeconomy and Discipline: officership and administration in the British army 1714–63* (Manchester, 1985).

32 D. Baugh, *Naval Administration, 1715–1750* (1977); Black and P. L. Woodfine eds., *The British Navy and the Use of Naval Power in the Eighteenth Century* (Leicester, 1988).

33 M. Fissell, *Patients, Power, and the Poor in Eighteenth-Century Bristol* (Cambridge, 1992).

34 Black, *Pitt the Elder* (Cambridge, 1992), pp. 19–21.

35 L. K. J. Glassey, 'Local government', in C. Jones ed., *Britain in the First Age of Party 1680–1750* (1987), p. 171; on excise administration, Brewer, *The Sinews of Power: war, money and the English state 1688–1783* (1989), pp. 101–14; E. Moir, *Local Government in Gloucestershire 1775–1800* (Bristol, 1969); B. Keith-Lucas, *The Unreformed Local Government System* (1980); N. Landau, *Justices of the Peace, 1679–1760* (Berkeley, 1984).

36 M. Turner and D. Mills eds., *Land and Property: the English land tax 1692–1832* (Gloucester, 1986); R. Davey, *East Sussex Land Tax 1785* (Lewes, 1991); D. E. Ginter, *A Measure of Wealth: the English land tax in historical analysis* (1992).

37 M. G. Smith, *Fighting Joshua* (Redruth, 1985) studies Trelawny as Bishop, Vice Admiral and borough monger.

38 R. Browning, *The Duke of Newcastle* (New Haven, 1975); R. Middleton, 'The Duke of Newcastle and the conduct of patronage during the Seven Years War, 1757–1762', *British Journal for Eighteenth-Century Studies*, XII (1985), pp. 175–86.

39 B. Philips, *Peterwell* (Aldershot, 1983).

40 Thomas, 'Plas Newyndd', p. 160.

41 E. Gregg, *Queen Anne* (1980); R. Hatton, *George I* (1978); J. B. Owen, 'George II reconsidered', in A. Whiteman, J. S. Bromley and P. G. M. Duckson, eds., *Statesmen, Scholars and Merchants* (Oxford, 1973), pp. 113–34.

42 Black, *A System of Ambition? British foreign policy 1660–1793* (1991), pp. 12–42.

43 Smith, *Men of No Property*, p. 33; V. A. Hatley, 'The headless trunk: a study in Northampton politics, 1795–96', *Northamptonshire Past and Present* VIII (1990–1) no. 2, p. 117.

44 Bolingbroke to Sir William Trumbull, 21 August 1702, Reading, Berkshire CRO. Additional Trumbull papers 133 9/1, now in BL.

2

The course of politics

The principal political threats to the Protestant succession and the Whig system were seen as coming from Jacobitism until mid-century, and from France. James II was succeeded in 1701 by the 'warming pan baby', 'James III', and, though the latter's attempt to invade Scotland with French support in 1708 was abortive,[1] his claim was a threat to the Hanoverian succession. The childless William III (1689–1702) had been succeeded by his sister-in-law Anne (1702–14), none of whose many children survived to adulthood. Under the Act of Settlement (1701), she was to be succeeded by the German house of Hanover, Protestant descendants of James I's daughter Elizabeth. The succession played a major role in the complex politics of the reigns of William III and Anne, being related to such divisive issues as ecclesiastical governance, toleration, foreign policy and military strategy. In the reign of William the Tory–Whig polarity had been confused by a Country–Court opposition. In the late-1690s the Country Whigs were largely absorbed by the Tories, so that a Whig–Tory division was central to the reign of Anne.

The peaceful accession of George I in 1714 was a major disappointment for James. The threat of a Jacobite rebellion had been taken seriously, but, largely as a result of inadequate Jacobite preparations and a refusal of several senior possible backers to provide support, this potential danger was avoided in 1714. The consequences were not, however, completely unhelpful for the Jacobites, for George's enthusiastic support of the Whigs, who did very well in the general election of 1715, alienated the Tories whom Anne had favoured in her last years and helped to revive Jacobitism. This led to risings in Scotland and northern England in 1715, but they were both defeated. The death of Louis XIV deprived the Jacobites of any hopes of getting even arms, if not troops, from France, and, after the arrest of the leaders of the proposed rising in the West of England, James sent orders to countermand the rebellion, but the Earl of Mar started it in Scotland without waiting to hear from James. The rebellion, known as the '15, lent fresh energy to the purge of Tories. They were excluded from most senior posts in government, the armed forces, the judiciary and the Church. In 1719 there was to be an unsuccessful Spanish invasion of Scotland on behalf of the Jacobites and in 1722 the Atterbury Plot, a plan to seize London, was blocked by prompt governmental action, including the creation of a large army camp in Hyde Park.[2] The 1720s and 1730s were bleak years for the Stuart cause, because the leading minister, the venal but able Sir Robert Walpole (1721–42), followed policies that were less aggressive and objectionable to the Tories than the Stanhope/Sunderland Whig ministry of 1717–20 and crucially kept Britain at peace for most of the period, thus denying the Jacobites foreign support. Except for the Tithe Bill in 1736, Walpole was unwilling to support any further improvement in the legal position of Dissenters, a measure that threatened the position of the Church of England and its Tory supporters in the localities. Walpole was certainly corrupt and his ministry was a Whig monopoly of power, but he caused offence principally to those who took a close interest in politics, rather than to the wider political nation, whose position was eased by his generally successful determination to reduce taxation, especially on land. In the Church, however, Walpole's policies were hindered because he was too exclusive in his use of patronage. He tried to avoid accommodating moderate (i.e. loyal) Tories, such as Thomas Sherlock.[3]

The Walpolean system broke down, however, in his last years. The collapse of Anglo-Spanish relations over vigorous Spanish policing of what they claimed was illegal British trade with their Caribbean possessions, symbolised by the display to a committee of the House of Commons of the allegedly severed ear of a merchant captain, Robert Jenkins, led to war (1739–48), a war that Walpole had sought to avoid. Initially the war united the country, but a lack of success, combined with poor relations between George II and Frederick, Prince of Wales, gravely weakened Walpole politically. He did very badly in the general election of 1741 and his inability to continue to command majorities in the Commons led to his fall in February 1742 (Doc. 3). The ministry, under the dynamic leadership of John, Lord Carteret, that replaced that led by Walpole sent British troops to the Continent in 1742 in order to resist French advances.

Britain had already fought France in 1689–97 (War of the League of Augsburg or Nine Years' War) and 1702–13 (War of the Spanish Succession). These wars were designed both to prevent Louis XIV's domination of western Europe and to safeguard the Protestant Succession. William III had only limited success in the 1690s, but John, Duke of Marlborough, the husband of Queen Anne's cantankerous favourite, Sarah Churchill, won a series of crushing victories (Blenheim 1704, Ramillies 1706, Oudenarde 1708, Malplaquet, 1709), that drove French forces out of Germany and the Low Countries. George I was able to negotiate an alliance (1716–31) with the regency government that followed Louis XIV, committing France to support, or at least accept, the Hanoverian succession, and Walpole kept the peace with France; but his successor's abandonment of this policy led to French support for Jacobitism. In 1743 the British defeated the French at Dettingen, George II being the last British king to command in battle, but in 1744 the French responded with a planned invasion of England on behalf of the Jacobites, only to be blocked by Channel storms.

The following year 'James III's' eldest son, Charles Edward (Bonnie Prince Charlie) evaded British warships and landed in the Western Isles. He quickly overran most of Scotland, despite the reluctance of some Jacobite clans to rise for a prince who had brought no soldiers, and the hostility of the many Scots who were not Jacobites. The British force in Scotland was outmanoeuvred and then fell victim to a Highland charge at Prestonpans outside Edinburgh (21 September 1745). Crossing into England on 8 November 1745, Charles Edward took Carlisle after a brief siege, and then, without any resistance, Lancaster, Preston, Manchester and Derby, which was entered on 4 December. The British armies had been outmanoeuvred and, if few English Jacobites had risen to help Charles, his opponents were affected by panic and a lack of support. The Jacobite council, however, decided on 5 December to retreat, despite Charles's wish to press on. The lack of English and French support weighed most heavily with the Highland chiefs. There had been a crucial breakdown of confidence in the prince among his supporters, arising from the failure of his promises over support. The Scots considered themselves as having been tricked into a risky situation.

Had the Jacobites pressed on, they might have won, capturing London and thus destroying the logistical and financial infrastructure of their opponents. By retreating they made defeat almost certain, not least because, in combination with bad weather and the British navy, the retreat led the French to abandon a planned supporting invasion of southern England. Charles evaded pursuit, retreated to Scotland successfully and on 17 January 1746 beat a British army at Falkirk; but George II's inexorable second son, William, Duke of Cumberland, brought up a formidable army and on Culloden Moor near Inverness on 16 April 1746 his superior firepower smashed the Jacobite army. Cumberland recorded of his opponents that 'in their rage that they could not make any impression upon the battalions, they threw stones at them for at least a minute or two, before their total rout began'. He had secured the Protestant Succession established by William III.

The aftermath was harsh. The Hanoverian regime had been temporarily overthrown in Scotland, the army humiliated, and the government was determined to ensure that there was no repetition of the '45. The Highlanders were regarded as barbarians, and Cumberland's successor, William, 2nd Earl of Albemarle, offered his solution for 'the bad inclination of the people in most of the northern counties and their stubborn, inveterate disposition of mind . . . nothing could effect it but laying the whole country waste and in ashes, and removing all the inhabitants (excepting a few) out of the kingdom'. The 'pacification' of the Highlands was to be characterised first by killings, rapes and systematic devastation, and secondly by a determined attempt to alter the political, social and strategic structure of the Highlands. The clans were disarmed, and the clan system broken up, while roads to open up the Highlands and forts to awe them were constructed. Hereditable jurisdictions were abolished, the wearing of Highland clothes prohibited. The rebellion and its suppression therefore gave cause and opportunity for the sort of radical state-directed action against inherited privilege, especially regional and aristocratic privilege, that was so rare in Britain.

More long-term political changes were also important. In effect Scotland, like many dependent parts of multiple kingdoms or federal states, was losing its capacity for important independent political initiatives. This affected both the Highlands and the country as a whole. It was not a case of English pressure on an unwilling people, for political changes profited, and were in part shaped by, local politicians. Many Scots were firm opponents of the Stuarts and supporters of the Protestant Succession. London relied on Scottish politicians not Englishmen sent to govern Scotland.[4] Jacobite conspiracies continued and contemporaries were still concerned about the situation: in the 1750s there was anxiety about Jacobite feeling in Oxford and Oxfordshire. Nevertheless, the strategic situation had altered greatly as a result of the crushing of Scottish Jacobitism, and support for James III in England appeared increasingly marginal and inconsequential.

The '45 had both revealed the vulnerability of, and led to the firm establishment of, the Hanoverian regime. It thus closed a long period of instability and, instead, provided the basis for a fundamental recasting of British politics in which Toryism lost its Jacobite aspect, thus facilitating the dissolution of the Whig–Tory divide over the following seventeen years. Attempts to conciliate and comprehend opponents within ministerial ranks, and expectations concerning the future behaviour of the heir to the throne, first Frederick Prince of Wales, who died in 1751, and then the future George III, along with the behaviour of the latter after he came to the throne in 1760, compromised the cohesion and identity of the Tories, and brought some of them into government. Co-operation in the localities between Whigs and Tories increased after the '45. In addition, the relationship between England and Scotland became essentially one of the willing co-option of the powerful Scots through patronage, with no alternative Jacobite or nationalist focus of loyalty and with a diminishing emphasis on coercion.

The unification of Britain helped her in conflict with France. The decisive struggle was the Seven Years' War (1756–63). It ended with the Thirteen Colonies on the eastern seaboard of North America, and the British possessions in India secure, with Canada, Florida, and many Caribbean islands acquired, and with Britain as the leading maritime power in the world, thus fulfilling what James Thomson had seen as the national destiny in his ode 'Rule Britannia' (1740): 'Rule Britannia, rule the waves: / Britons never will be slaves.' This was the achievement of the ministry of William Pitt the Elder and the Duke of Newcastle (1757–61), and of a number of able military leaders, including Wolfe, Clive, Hawke and Boscawen.[5] Robert Clive's victory at Plassey, over the vastly more numerous forces of the Indian Prince, Surajah Dowla, in 1757, laid the basis for the virtual control of Bengal, Bihar and Orissa by the East India Company. The French were subjugated in India in 1760–1, and Britain emerged as the most powerful European state in the Indian subcontinent. The French attempt to invade Britain on behalf of the Jacobites was crushed by the British naval victories of Lagos and Quibéron Bay (1759). That year, British troops also beat the French at Minden in Germany, while, after a hazardous ascent of the cliffs near Quebec, the city was captured, General James Wolfe dying at the moment of glorious victory on the Plains of Abraham. The bells of victory rang out across Britain: the ringers at York Minster were paid four times between 21 August and 22 October for celebrating triumphs, beginning with Minden and ending with Quebec. The victories were also a tribute to the national unity that had followed the defeat of Jacobitism: a Highland charge played a major role at Quebec. In 1762 British forces campaigned round the globe. They helped the Portuguese resist a Spanish invasion, fought the French in Germany and captured Martinique from the French and Havana and Manila from the Spaniards, an extraordinary testimony to the global reach of British power and the strength of the British state.

Britain was soon to have to defend its maritime and colonial position from serious challenges, rebellion in America and Ireland, war with Revolutionary and Napoleonic France. The society that did so was changing both socially and economically. After a century of limited growth, if not stagnation, population growth rates shot up, leading to a rise in the population of England and Wales from about 6 million in 1742 to 8.2 million in 1789. Though real wages suffered and Britain had to import grain in significant quantities in bad years such as 1766 to feed the growing numbers, this greater population was sustained and high growth rates continued. A decline in the death rate was less important than an increase in fertility from the 1780s to the 1820s. Agricultural improvement, the construction of canals and better roads, and the development of industry and trade led to a growth in national wealth and a different economy, so that the percentage of the male labour force employed in industry rose from 19 (1700) to 30 (1800), while that in agriculture fell from 60 to 40, though agricultural productivity increased. In order to facilitate a reorganisation of the rural landscape that enhanced the control and profits of landlords, 1,532 enclosure Acts were passed between 1760 and 1797. In 1790 the Oxford Canal reached Oxford, creating the final link in a network joining the rivers Trent, Mersey and Thames.[6]

Even if the rate of industrialisation was less impressive than used to be believed, the qualitative impact of economic change was obvious to contemporaries. The impression was of Prometheus Unbound, of extraordinary opportunities offered by technological innovation, as exemplified in the report in the *Darlington Pamphlet* of 1772 that 'an ingenious mechanic has just invented a machine with which a girl of ten years of age may spin several threads'. John Kay's flying shuttle of 1733, which was in general use in Yorkshire by the 1780s, increased the productivity of handloom weavers. James Hargreaves's spinning jenny (1768), Richard Arkwright's waterframe (1769) and Samuel Crompton's mule (1779) revolutionised textile spinning. In 1769 James Watt patented a more energy-efficient use of steam engines. Greater ease of communication helped to unify the élite, facilitating education, socialising and travel for business or political reasons. London newspapers were sent to the provinces in increasing numbers, and postal services improved considerably, Royal Mail coach services starting in 1784, to the benefit of the expanding banking system as well as to the letter writer, that central character in two recent and rapidly developing literary forms, the novel and the magazine. The critical 'political' aspect of these economic changes was that, in contrast to the situation on the Continent, they owed relatively little to governmental sponsorship. Parliament passed the necessary legislation, but it did so, essentially, as a cockpit for local interests. A favourable tariff regime was not the same as the use of governmental resources for new canals or factories.

Many of the social features that were to be associated with economic transformation were already common. Far from Britain being a rural elysium, lacking a Boucher to depict plenty and languorous calm but all too soon to be ravaged by industrialisation, the rural world had already in 1500–1640 witnessed massive disruptions of land and labour. Neither enclosure, sweeping changes in land use, rural proletarianisation nor the social and economic changes wrought by industrialisation, technological change and the rise and decline of specific areas and economic activities were new; though they were both to increase in scale and pace from the late eighteenth century, and never to cease to do so thereafter. This process of continual change, more than anything else, marked the birth of modern times. The social changes of the period were, however, disruptive. Enclosure served principally to increase landlord rents and was often accompanied by the shedding of labour, leading to rural unemployment, pauperisation and hardship. The extent to which there was a peasantry with a proprietory interest in the soil was reduced.[7] This loss of security of tenure increased uncertainty, not least by dislocating the senses of place and identity for many who worked on the land. At the same time, changes in urban employment as a result of economic developments, were also disruptive.

For those who wielded power, however, political, not social or economic, challenges were foremost. Indeed, the material condition of the population played only a slight role in politics. This was not to alter significantly until the 1790s when concern about possible revolution led to more awareness of the consequences of material circumstances. Prior to that, issues such as food prices and wages played only an episodic role in high politics.

The Whig–Tory two-party system was replaced in the 1760s by a number of essentially personal political groups, the rivalries of political leaders and the changing preferences of George III (1760–1820)[8] fostering instability. Aside from a new king, there was also a new generation of political leaders, as well as new issues. In combination, these ensured a very different political situation. It could be argued that the years 1720–60 were really dominated by the personal factionalism of Walpole and the Pelhams, which looked like a party because of their longevity in power. If such an approach is adopted, then there was less a change to the politics of personal factions from 1760 than a case of factions swapping places frequently. The crucial division between Tories and opposition Whigs and the role of issues, on which there were recognisable party positions, in the politics of the first half of the century suggests, however, that it is appropriate to adopt a party approach to the politics of the period.

As much as any Continental ruler who did not have to face a powerful representative institution, George was determined to reject what he saw as the politics of faction, to thwart the efforts of unacceptable politicians to force their way into office. Like other rulers, George found it most difficult to create acceptable relationships with senior politicians at his accession, when he had to persuade those who had had a good working relationship with his predecessor, and those who had looked for a dramatic change, to adjust to his wishes. George broke with Pitt in 1761 and Newcastle in 1762 and made his favourite, John, 3rd Earl of Bute, First Lord of the Treasury in 1762, only to see the weak-willed Bute resign in 1763 in the face of bitter domestic opposition. George complained to the French ambassador in 1763 about 'the spirit of fermentation and the excessive licence which prevails in England. It is essential to neglect nothing that can check that spirit.'[9] The ambiguity of a number of constitutional points, such as the collective responsibility of the Cabinet and the degree to which the monarch had to choose his ministers from those who had the confidence of Parliament, exacerbated the situation.[10] Not until 1770 did George find a satisfactory minister who could control Parliament: Frederick, Lord North.

The volatile political atmosphere in London also contributed to a sense of crisis in the 1760s. Dissatisfaction there was exploited by a squinting anti-hero John Wilkes, an entrepreneur of faction and libertine MP, who fell foul of George III as a result of bitter attacks on the government in his newspaper the *North Briton*. Wilkes's denunciation in number 45 (23 April 1763) of the Peace of Paris led to a charge of seditious libel. The article implied that George III had lied in his speech from the throne. The government took a number of contentious steps, issuing a general warrant for the arrest of all those involved in the publication of number 45 and seeking to arrest Wilkes, despite his parliamentary privilege. Though released, Wilkes, later in 1763, was accused of blasphemy because he attributed his indecent *Essay on Woman* to a cleric. The Commons resolved that seditious libel was not covered by parliamentary privilege and in 1764 Wilkes was expelled and, eventually, outlawed. Wilkes's expulsion was exploited by opposition politicians keen to throw doubts on the legality of ministerial actions. In 1768 he returned to England and was elected for Middlesex. Wilkes was imprisoned for blasphemy and libel and expelled from the Commons. Three times re-elected by Middlesex in 1769, he was declared incapable of being re-elected by Parliament and his opponent was declared elected, a thwarting of the views of the electors that aroused anger. Wilkes was the focus of more widespread popular opposition to the government and a measure of radicalism that led in 1768 to a series of riots in London.[11] As with the Chartist movement in the 1840s, radicalism owed something to economic problems.

Britain after 1763 was a much wealthier and more self-confident nation, but one facing a new set of problems, notably issues of imperial government and finance. The role of the British state in the affairs of the East India Company and the protection of British India increased appreciably and this proved a source of considerable controversy. American affairs proved more politically charged, not least because of the large number of British emigrants in North America and the close links with the British economy.

The discontent and divisions of the 1760s over the determination of George III to pick ministers of his own choice and other issues paled into insignificance beside the collapse of the imperial relationship with America. The determination to make colonies, not represented in Parliament, pay a portion of their defence burden was crucial to the conflict, though so also was the increasing democratization in American society, a millenarian rejection of British authority, concern about British policy in Canada, and the borrowing of British conspiracy theories about the supposed autocratic intentions of George III.[12] The fact that neither Canada nor Britain's most important colonies in the western hemisphere, those in the West Indies, rebelled, despite the sensitivity of their élites on questions of constitutional principle, suggests that it was the increasingly serious social, economic and

political crises in the American colonies that were crucial.[13] After
the controversy caused by the Stamp Act of 1765, the Revenue
Act of 1767 drawn up by Charles Townshend imposed American
customs duties on a variety of goods including tea, which was
brought from India by the East India Company. It led to a serious
deterioration in relations between the British government and its
American critics. The latter responded with a trade boycott and
action against customs officials, leading the British ministry to
send troops to Boston in 1768.[14] In 1769 the government decided
to abandon all the Townshend duties save that on tea, whose
retention was seen as a necessary demonstration that it would
not yield to colonial agitation. Relations remained poor, with
serious constitutional disputes of varied cause in a number of
colonies, particular tension in Massachusetts and a growing hostility towards parliamentary claims to authority over American
affairs. The Boston Tea Party of 16 December 1773 arose from
American fears that the authorities would seize boycotted tea
and force its sale. About sixty men raided three ships in Boston
Harbour and dumped the contents of 340 chests of tea into the
sea. This forced the government to confront the growing problems of law and order and the maintenance of authority. They
believed these arose from the actions of a small number in
America, rather than from widespread disaffection, and thus
mistakenly hoped that tough action against Massachusetts, the
so-called Coercive or Intolerable Acts of early 1774, would lead
to the restoration of order. The Boston Port Act was designed to
protect trade and customs officials from harassment, the Administration of Justice and Quartering Acts to make it easier to enforce order. These measures were criticised by the opposition in
Britain as oppressive, but passed by overwhelming majorities.
Parliamentary sovereignty over the Thirteen Colonies was generally supported and there was widespread backing for a policy
of firmness. More troops were sent to Massachusetts.[15]

Fighting broke out near Boston in April 1775 as a result of the
determination of the government of Lord North to employ force
to secure its authority, and the willingness of sufficient Americans to do likewise in order to resist British authority. The
Americans declared independence (1776) and the British were
driven from the bulk of the Thirteen Colonies but held Canada
(1775 to spring 1776), before counter-attacking to regain New

York (1776). The British seizure of Philadelphia was matched by defeat at Saratoga (1777), and after the French entered the war on the revolutionary side (1778), the British lacked the resources necessary for sustaining their earlier scale of offensive operations in America and were pushed on to the defensive in a world war. Spain joined France in 1779 and at the end of 1780 the Dutch were added to the list of Britain's enemies in what was truly a global conflict.

Though the Franco-Spanish attempt to invade England failed (1779), and the British held on to Gibraltar, India and Jamaica, defeat at Yorktown (1781) was followed by the acceptance of American independence.[16] This split the unity of the English-speaking world. America, inhabited by an independent people of extraordinary vitality, was to be the most dynamic of the independent states in the western hemisphere, the first and foremost of the decolonised countries, the people that were best placed to take advantage of the potent combination of a European legacy, independence, and the opportunities for expansion and growth that were to play an increasingly important role in the new world created from 1776. America was to ensure that aspects of British culture, society and ideology, albeit in altered forms, were to enjoy great influence, outside and after the span of British empire, but to contemporaries the signs of British defeat, decline and division seemed clear.

As so often in British history, defeat led to the fall of the government. Lord North's resignation in 1782 was followed by a period of marked ministerial and constitutional instability. George was forced to accept ministers whom he disliked, threatened abdication, and in 1783–4 breached several fundamental political conventions in engineering the fall of the Fox–North ministry and supporting that of the twenty-four-year-old William Pitt the Younger (Prime Minister 1783–1801, 1804–6), the severe but sometimes drunk second son of Pitt the Elder, although it lacked a Commons majority. Pitt's victory in the 1784 general election was also therefore a triumph for George and it began a period of generally stable government that lasted until Pitt's resignation in 1801. Like Walpole and North, Pitt understood the importance of sound finances, and, although he was interested in electoral reform, he did not push this divisive issue after it had been defeated in 1785. As so often in a monarchical state, continuity was, however, threatened by the succession, for George III's eldest son, George, later George IV, was opposed not only to the frugality, virtue and duty of his father, but also to Pitt, preferring instead the latter's opponent, Charles James Fox, who, unlike the Prince, had talent, but, like him, lacked self-control. When in late 1788 an attack of porphyria led to the conviction that George III was mad, the resulting Regency Crisis nearly produced the fall of the government. Fortunately for Pitt, the king recovered in early 1789.[17]

Defeat at the hands of America had led to reform, especially in the Royal Navy, and this was to help Britain in the more serious challenge that lay ahead. She recovered from the loss of the Thirteen Colonies, Florida and various Caribbean islands (Treaty of Versailles, 1783), to establish the first British foothold in Malaysia (Penang 1786) and the first European colony in Australia (1788), and to thwart Spanish attempts to prevent her from trading and establishing settlements on the western coast of modern Canada (Nootka Sound crisis, 1790). In contrast, the French took a long time to recover from their subsequent loss during the Revolutionary–Napoleonic period of maritime power and colonial possessions and pretensions, while Spain did not recover from the loss of her Latin American empire in the early nineteenth century.

Though buffeted seriously during the war with Revolutionary and then Napoleonic France (1793–1802, 1803–14, 1815), most worryingly with the Irish rising of 1798 and the threat of invasion by Napoleon from 1803, Britain survived, thanks in particular to a series of naval victories, culminating in Nelson's apotheosis at Trafalgar (1805). The war against Revolutionary France had revealed, however, that the British were unable to defend the Low Countries, and subsequent expeditions there, the 1799 landing in Holland under George III's son Frederick, Duke of York (now best remembered in a nursery rhyme for marching troops up and down hills), and the 1809 attack on Walcheren, ended in failure. Napoleon's domination of the Continent was a major challenge to British interests. He sought in the Continental System, which was inaugurated in November 1806, to bring Britain to her knees by economic means. The Berlin Decrees declared Britain blockaded and banned trade with her. Napoleon's extra-European interests were also a threat to Britain. His invasion of Egypt in 1798 had been gravely weakened when Horatio Nelson destroyed the French fleet at the Battle of the Nile in Aboukir Bay, but, thereafter, Napoleon remained interested in the prospect of weakening the British in India, possibly in co-operation with Russia, and of establishing new French colonies.[18]

The war placed a major strain on British resources, and defeats led to or exacerbated political problems. Pitt the Younger discovered that wartime leadership was considerably more difficult than the period of reform and regeneration he had earlier helped to orchestrate, and he died, worn out, in office. The cost and economic disruption of the war pressed hard throughout society, leading to the introduction of income tax (1799), the stagnation of average real wages and to widespread hardship, especially in the famine years of 1795–6 and 1799–1801. Radicals found their activities prohibited or limited, while trade unions were hindered, though not ended, by the Combination Acts of 1799 and 1800 which made combinations for improved pay or conditions illegal.[19] Further economic difficulties arose from the war with the United States of America (1812–14) over the British regulation of neutral trade. The British burnt Washington and defended Canada successfully, but were defeated outside New Orleans. That conflict, the only war Britain fought with the United States after 1783, was only a diversion, however, from the struggle with Napoleon. Eventual triumph in that came as part of an alliance to which Britain contributed money (£66 million in subsidies and armaments to her allies), and the Duke of Wellington's victories in Portugal and Spain in the Peninsular War (1808–13), such as Vimeiro (1808), Talavera (1809), Salamanca (1812), and Vitoria (1813). The disciplined firepower of the British infantry played a major part in these triumphs. Wellington never had more than 40,000 British troops under his personal command and was always outnumbered in both cavalry and artillery, but he was a fine judge of terrain and, as at Vimeiro, the well-positioned British lines succeeded in blunting the attacking French columns. British commitment culminated in the major roles taken at the Congress of Vienna and, under Wellington, on the battlefield of Waterloo (1815). Though British troops composed less than half of the Anglo-German-Dutch force that Wellington commanded, they played a decisive role in stopping the successive advances of French cavalry and infantry, until finally Napoleon's veteran Guard units were driven back and the arrival of Prussian troops helped to tip the balance against the French.

Naval power permitted Britain to dominate the European trans-oceanic world during the Revolutionary and Napoleonic wars. Danish, Dutch, French and Spanish naval power were crippled; Britain was left free to execute amphibious attacks on the now-isolated centres of other European powers, and to make gains at the expense of non-European peoples. The route to India was secured: Cape Town was captured in 1795 and then again, after it had been restored in 1802, in 1806, the Seychelles in 1794, Réunion and Mauritius in 1810. The British position in India and Australasia was consolidated, while her gains at the Congress of Vienna included Ceylon, the Seychelles, Mauritius, Trinidad, Tobago, St Lucia, Malta, Cape Colony and Guiana. Britain replaced Spain as the major power in the Pacific, while India served as the basis of British control and influence around the Indian Ocean.

The nature of the British empire and of the European world both altered dramatically. In 1775 the majority of British subjects outside Britain were white (though the population of the West Indian colonies were predominantly black slaves), Christian, of British, or at least European, origin, and ruled with an element of local self-government. By 1815 none of this was true. By then most of the trans-oceanic European world outside the western hemisphere was British; by 1830 this was true of the vast majority of all European possessions abroad. The situation was not to last; indeed 1830 was the date of the French occupation of Algiers, the basis of their subsequent North African empire. Nevertheless the unique imperial oceanic position that Britain occupied in the Revolutionary, Napoleonic and post-Napoleonic period was to be of crucial importance to its nineteenth-century economic and cultural development. France was to become a great imperial power again; Portugal and the Dutch were to make gains, Germany, Italy, Belgium (and the United States) to become imperial powers. Yet for none of these was empire as important, as central a feature of public culture, as it was for Britain, by the late Victorian and Edwardian period. The rise in British imperial power had a great influence on the British economy, and on the British élite, who were provided with a new sense of role and mission and, in many cases, with careers. Service in the colonies, particularly in India, came to be prestigious, more so than anything similar in France or Germany. The sense of Britain playing a major role in resisting challenges to the European system, which had characterised opposition to Louis XIV, the Revolution and Napoleon, ebbed, as empire, especially from the mid and late 1870s, set the themes of Britain's role and identity, a process that was furthered by the development of widespread emigration to certain colonies. The establishment of the British imperial position owed much to success in war, and it was not surprising that the pantheon of imperial heroes defined and depicted in the nineteenth century was largely composed of naval and military figures, such as Nelson. Wellington, 'the last great Englishman' according to the Poet Laureate, Alfred Tennyson (1852), was the only former general in British history to become Prime Minister (1828–30, 1834): James, 1st Viscount Stanhope's position in 1716–21 does not merit the description.

It is clear from this survey that a crucial component of eighteenth-century *British* politics, both domestic and foreign, was naval and military force, and yet this has never been considered by the political historians of the period. There are three reasons for this. First, most work has concentrated on English history, has, if it has considered British questions, done so from an English viewpoint, and has been written by English scholars; and in the history of England (as opposed to Britain) in this period, military force played a relatively modest role after 1688. There was nothing to compare with the role of force in suppressing the Irish rising of 1798. Second, political historians are commonly disinclined to write about military questions, not least because they dislike the element of uncertainty and chance that military conflict produces. Third, there has been a tendency in discussing the British dimension to focus on the cultural, ideological and other factors leading to closer relations within Britain, or at least to the creation of a British élite. Such explanations tend, however, to neglect military factors, recalling R. J. W. Evans's emphasis on the appeal of Catholic, baroque and 'absolutist' values in explaining Austrian strength in the seventeenth century.[20] They reflect the recently influential notions of cultural hegemony that have also influenced assessments of how notions of justice and law were used to keep order in eighteenth-century England, a society that was very lightly policed. In contrast, Linda Colley's recent emphasis, in explaining the development of an eighteenth-century British consciousness on war, alongside common Protestantism and the shared benefits of empire, is pertinent.[21]

Recent work on the mid seventeenth century has made it clear that the English Civil Wars have to be seen as British conflicts[22] and that the British dimension had a direct impact on the course (and in some cases cause) of developments in England. Thus, far from seeing the struggles in Ireland and Scotland in 1689–1746 as simple after-shocks of the Glorious Revolution in England, as the inevitable extension into less central regions of a political settlement that had already been determined in England, it is necessary to emphasise their importance for English history. Jacobitism posed a question mark not only against the dynastic changes of 1689 and 1714 (the latter more clearly and crucially a product of parliamentary action, the Act of Settlement of 1701, than that of 1689 had been), but also against the changes in the relationships between England, Ireland and Scotland that had occurred in this period, and against the clear establishment of a parliamentary monarchy.

The defeat of Jacobitism required military force, not only in the actual campaigns, but also in the preventing or thwarting of Jacobite conspiracies, such as the Atterbury Plot in 1722. A considerable military effort was devoted to preventing rebellion in Scotland and Ireland. General George Wade, Commander-in-Chief in Scotland 1724–40, constructed a network of military roads so that his forces could nip any rising in the bud. In 1729 he wrote from Dalnacardok in the Highlands, 'though the Jacobites are more numerous here than in any other part of His Majesty's dominions, by the present disposition of forces it seems to me impracticable for them to give any disturbance to the government unless supported by troops from abroad'. In 1746 the Duke of Cumberland closed his report on Culloden by writing 'It will be absolutely necessary, that new forts be erected here [Inverness], and where Fort Augustus stood'.[23] His successor, Albemarle, was part of the Anglo-Dutch aristocracy created by that latter-day William the Conqueror, William III: the Bentincks becoming Dukes of Portland, the Keppels Earls of Albemarle, the Nassaus Earls of Grantham, the Zuylesteins Earls of Rochford. Rather like a Norman noble sent to hold the Welsh or Scottish marches, he outlined a system of military-based rule to the Duke of Newcastle in October 1746 (Doc. 4). The eighteenth-century British state was not one given to expensive programmes of fortress construction, at least in Britain, though the situation was different in some overseas bases, such as Gibraltar. In 1746, however, William Skinner was sent to Scotland, as chief engineer of North Britain, to build defensive works that could control the Highlands. He proposed a major new fort near Inverness at Arderseer Point. This Fort George cost over £100,000 to build. A 'state-of-the-art' bastioned fortification, it remains to this day an impressive work. Existing bases, such as Fort William, were improved, while a new barracks was constructed at Edinburgh, which Albemarle hoped would lessen the need to billet men and thus expose them to the Jacobite sympathies of the natives. Wade's road programme was extended, Albemarle being ordered in August 1746 to use troops in order to complete the road from Dunbarton to the Western Isles as soon as possible. On the basis of a military survey, Scotland was mapped.

The ravelins of Fort George have never before been seen as a symbol of eighteenth-century British politics but they are an apt one for two reasons. First, they symbolised the determination of successive governments to enforce the dominance of the policies and politics of the ruling élite throughout the British Isles; their realisation that their security required this, a crucial lesson from the mid-seventeenth-century crisis; and their awareness that this security could be obtained only if the links between domestic and international opposition were broken. Fort George, which never heard a shot fired in anger, was designed to resist any amphibious attack on Inverness and the Great Glen from the Moray Firth. English governments had for centuries suffered from foreign intervention either in domestic English politics or in support of opponents within the British Isles. Thus, the French had supported John's opponents, as well as invasions against Edward IV and Richard III, their Burgundian rivals backing invasions against Henry VI and Henry VII. France had backed Scotland in the War of Independence against England and thereafter; Philip III of Spain had in 1601 sent troops to help Irish resistance to Elizabeth I. English governments had been able only to push through unpopular domestic changes, such as the Henrician and Edwardian Reformations, or crush opposition within

Britain, as Henry VIII had fitfully sought, and as parliamentary forces had done in 1648–51, if potential Continental opponents, such as France, which was far more populous, were occupied in war.

From 1688 the situation altered as Britain came to play a more major role in European warfare, though that encouraged foreign rivals to plan intervention on behalf of domestic opponents of the British government. Thus France in 1692, 1696, 1708, 1744–6 and 1759, and Spain in 1719 prepared to invade on behalf of the Jacobites, and from 1793 the government of Revolutionary France sought to sponsor British radicalism, sending forces to invade Wales and Ireland.[24] The British troops that fought France on Continental battlefields, the warships that blockaded Brest and other French ports, were therefore in part helping to secure hegemony in Britain, to prevent the overturning not only of the Revolution Settlement but also of that central political 'achievement' of first 1648–51 and then 1688–1746: the common destiny of the constituent parts of the British Isles, the end of the independent political trajectories of Ireland and Scotland, an achievement that was sustained until the Anglo-Irish Treaty of 1921.

The second reason why Fort George is so apt is that it symbolised the power on which the political system rested. Eighteenth-century Britain, especially England, was not a militarised society. By European standards the army was small, and the most impressive aspect of Britain as a military power, her navy, was more segregated from society than if comparable resources had been expended on the army. An English tourist noted in 1735 that most castles 'are at present quite neglected'.[25] There was a strong prejudice against a 'standing' (permanent) army, a legacy of the use of troops by Cromwell and the Stuarts and a response to the fear that such a force could be used for arbitrary acts. Nevertheless, a standing army remained, and was used both for civil policing and to preserve the Protestant Succession, British unity and imperial power. In the last resort, force was the crucial political weapon, and many members of the élite were aware of their role in this context. The essential nature of a political system (if such a concept has meaning) can be revealed under pressure. This can be seen in the response to the Jacobites. Newcastle had raised a troop for service during the '15, his brother Henry Pelham, First Lord of the Treasury 1743–54, had

51

served that year as a volunteer at the battle of Preston, while William, 1st Earl of Harrington, Secretary of State for the Northern Department 1730–42, 1744–6, had been a colonel during the '15. The leading military role on the Hanoverian side during the '45 was taken by the Duke of Cumberland, and other aristocrats played a major role, Lieutenant-General Charles Lennox, 2nd Duke of Richmond as a cavalry general, the 3rd Earl of Cholmondeley as Governor of Chester Castle and Lord Lieutenant of Cheshire. The army was supplemented by allowing selected loyal aristocrats to raise regiments, and selected Lord Lieutenants were empowered to form their own military units.[26] During the War of American Independence, the domestic correspondence of Lord Amherst, who was in effect Commander-in-Chief of the army 1778–82, gives the impression of a society in which aristocratic Lords Lieutenant played a significant military function,[27] and as revolution seemed imminent in late 1792 there were echoes of the baronial past (Doc. 5).

And yet, at the same time, the Pitt government was to turn in other directions as it sought to recruit support. In place of the traditional reliance in England on billeting troops in inns and public houses, and thus ensuring that they lived 'among the people' rather than in what was seen as the militaristic practice of barracks, the government began in July 1792 a policy of purchasing or erecting barracks.[28] If reliance on the landed élite might appear conservative, the attempt to encourage a mass movement of loyalism by, for example, sponsoring favourable press treatment revealed a willingness to turn to and an ability to use the public politics of the period. The popularity of the governing regime was far greater in the 1790s than in the period of Old Corps Whiggery when opposition candidates were frequently elected by the more populous constituencies. The 1796 general election was a triumph for the government: 'Radical platforms were raised at Bristol, Colchester, London, Norwich, Nottingham and Westminster, to no effect.'[29]

And yet the attempt to secure and sustain a loyalist body politic in the 1790s was challenged by the upsurge in social and political radicalism. In 1792 Henry Dundas, the government's political manager in Scotland, warned Pitt that 'if the spirit of liberty and equality continues to spread with the same rapidity' it would be impossible to suppress sedition by force alone. He added, 'the safety of the country must I am persuaded depend on the body of the well affected to the Constitution (which with few exceptions is every body of property or respect) in some shape or other taking an open, active and declared part'.[30] It is therefore necessary to turn to this larger body, and to consider what made them well affected and how their views were communicated within the political system.

Notes

1 J. S. Gibson, *Playing the Scottish Card: the Franco-Jacobite invasion of 1708* (Edinburgh, 1988).

2 G. V. Bennett, *The Tory Crisis in Church and State 1688–1730: the career of Francis Atterbury* (Oxford, 1975).

3 Black, *Robert Walpole and the Nature of Politics in Early Eighteenth Century England* (1990); N. Sykes, *Edmund Gibson, Bishop of London* (Oxford, 1926).

4 Black, *Culloden and the '45* (Stroud, 1990).

5 Middleton, *The Bells of Victory: the Pitt–Newcastle Ministry and the conduct of the Seven Years War* (Cambridge, 1985).

6 W. Albert, *The Turnpike Road System in England 1663–1840* (Cambridge, 1972); E. Pawson, *Transport and Economy: the turnpike roads of eighteenth-century Britain* (1977); E. R. C. Hadfield, *British Canals* (6th ed., Newton Abbot, 1979); M. W. McCahill, *Order and Equipoise: the peerage and the House of Lords, 1783–1806* (1978), p. 90; R. G. Thorne ed., *The House of Commons 1790–1820* (5 vols., 1986), i, 337.

7 Turner, *English Parliamentary Enclosure: its historical geography and economic history* (Folkestone, 1980); R. C. Allen, *Enclosure and the Yeoman: the agricultural development of the South Midlands 1450–1850* (Oxford, 1992); J. M. Neeson, *Commoners: common right, enclosure and social change in England, 1700–1820* (Cambridge, 1993).

8 J. Brooke, *George III* (1972).

9 Duke of Nivernais to Duke of Praslin, French foreign minister, 11 May 1763, Paris, Ministère des Affaires Etrangères, Correspondance Politique Angleterre 450 fol. 337.

10 M. Peters, 'Pitt as a foil to Bute', in K. W. Schweizer ed., *Lord Bute: essays in re-interpretation* (Leicester, 1988), p. 111.

11 Brewer, *Party Ideology.*

12 B. Bailyn, *The Ideological Origins of the American Revolution* (Cambridge, Mass., 1967); R. J. Dinkin, *Voting in Provincial America: a study of elections in the Thirteen Colonies, 1689–1776* (Westport, 1977); N. O. Hatch, *The Sacred Cause of Liberty: republican thought and the mil-*

lenium in Revolutionary New England (New Haven, 1977).

13   T. R. Clayton, 'Sophistry, security and socio-political structures in the American Revolution, or why Jamaica did not rebel', *Historical Journal* XXIX (1986).

14   L. B. Namier and Brooke, *Charles Townshend* (1964), pp. 158–72; P. D. G. Thomas, *The Townshend Duties Crisis: the second phase of the American Revolution 1767–1773* (Oxford, 1987), pp. 18–36.

15   B. Donoughue, *British Politics and the American Revolution 1773–1775* (1984); Thomas, *Tea Party to Independence: the third phase of the American Revolution, 1773–1776* (Oxford, 1991).

16   Black, *War for America: the fight for American independence* (Stroud, 1991).

17   J. Ehrman, *The Younger Pitt* i (1969); J. W. Derry, *The Regency Crisis and the Whigs 1788–9* (Cambridge, 1963).

18   C. D. Hall, *British Strategy in the Napoleonic War* (Manchester, 1992).

19   Ehrman, *The Younger Pitt* ii (1983); Dickinson ed., *Britain and the French Revolution 1789–1815* (1989).

20   R. J. W. Evans, *The Making of the Habsburg Monarchy 1550–1700* (Oxford, 1979).

21   Colley, *Britons*.

22   C. Russell, *The Causes of the English Civil War* (Oxford, 1990), and *The Fall of the British Monarchies 1637–42* (Oxford, 1991).

23   Wade to Newcastle, 29 August 1729, PRO. SP. 54/19; HMC. *Reports on the Manuscripts of the Earls of Eglinton . . .* (1885), p. 444.

24   M. Elliott, *Partners in Revolution: the United Irishmen and France* (New Haven, 1982).

25   J. Dodd, tour, BL. Add. 5957 fo. 20.

26   P. Luff, 'The noblemen's regiments: politics and the 'forty-five', *Historical Research*, LXV (1992), pp. 54–73.

27   PRO. War Office corresp. vol. 34.

28   J. R. Breihan, 'Army barracks in the north-east in the era of the French Revolution', *Archaeologiana Aeliana*, 5th ser. XVIII (1990), pp. 165–76, 'Army barracks in Devon during the French Revolutionary and Napoleonic Wars', *Devon Association Report and Transactions*, CXXII (1990), pp. 133–58, 'Barracks in Dorset during the French Revolutionary and Napoleonic Wars', *Proceedings of the Dorset Natural History and Archaeological Society*, CXI (1989), pp. 9–14.

29   Thorne, *House of Commons*, i, 147–50.

30   Dundas to Pitt, 22 November 1792, PRO. 30/8/157 fos 142–3.

3

Political worlds

The political structure of Hanoverian Britain can be anatomised in formal terms, by means of a description of constitutional conventions, parliamentary rights and electoral arrangements,[1] as well as in the informal terms of patronage networks, the affinities of late medieval society in a new form. It is also possible to put diversity first not by turning to a descending system of government, one that traces the impacts, influences and networks of national institutions and politicians, but rather by beginning in the localities. There it is the diversity of society that is most apparent. Alongside the aspects of a national economy, suggested most obviously by the absence of internal tariffs within England, was the continued medley of local economies, the worlds of clay and chalk, arable and pastoral, dairying and sheep-and-corn, with all their varied social consequences in terms of settlement patterns, social practices and discipline. This diversity was related to political and religious variations. A recent study of Gloucestershire has argued that areas of rural industry were crucial sources of change in all respects, economic, political and religious. Economic diversity was in some respects lessened during the period, not least because of the communications revolution produced by the turnpiking of roads, improvement of coach services and river navigation and the development of canals; but these could also accentuate or create new differences, between for example regions that had good transport links and those that lacked them. As some regions industrialised, others, such as the West Country and East Anglia, experienced the opposite process.[2]

Diversity was also a characteristic of the electoral system. After the Act of Union of 1707, the House of Commons contained 558 MPs elected by 314 constituencies: forty English counties, 203 English boroughs, two English universities, twelve Welsh counties, twelve Welsh boroughs and forty-five Scottish constituencies. These categories were themselves far from uniform. The 203 English boroughs returned 405 MPs, the overwhelming majority of the House of Commons. Two boroughs, the City of London and the united boroughs of Weymouth and Melcombe Regis, returned four MPs each, 196 returned two each, and five returned one each. Voters were permitted to cast two votes, though they could choose to use only one. All the Welsh constituencies returned one MP each, but seven of the seats were groups of boroughs united for electoral purposes, one, Cardiff, containing eight boroughs. Twenty-seven of the thirty-three Scottish counties each sent one MP to the Commons, but the other six were grouped in pairs, one of each alternating with the other in electing MPs. Bar Edinburgh, the Scottish burghs were combined in groups in order to elect MPs.

The size of the electorate varied greatly in each category. Yorkshire had the largest electorate with 20,000 voters, while Sutherland, one of the larger Scottish counties, had only about ten voters in 1754. Even when the franchise (right of voting) was nominally the same there could be significant variations in the size of the electorate. In the first half of the century Kent had about 7,000 voters, Huntingdonshire about 1,500. The franchise, however, was far from uniform. Under a statute of 1429, the English counties theoretically all had the 40-shilling freehold: the possession (not necessarily ownership) of freehold property valued at 40 shillings per year. However both freehold and the 40-shilling value were open to various definitions. In early eighteenth-century Cheshire, for example, the term 'freehold' had to be mediated through a manorial structure with a complex lease and rental system: 40 shillings could refer to a property valuation for the land tax, to rent paid or to annual yield. The situation was, however, clarified by legislation in 1745 and 1780.[3]

The English borough franchise was consciously varied, with householder, freeman, scot and lot, corporation, burgage and freeholder boroughs. In the twelve householder or 'potwalloper' boroughs the right of voting was enjoyed by all inhabitants not receiving poor relief or charity. The qualifications for becoming freemen in the ninety-two freeman boroughs varied greatly, though generally the influence of the corporation over the creation of freemen ensured that its views had to be considered. The thirty-seven scot and lot constituencies gave the vote to inhabitant householders, so that occupation of property was crucial. In some of these constituencies it was necessary also to pay the poor rate; in others the franchise was enjoyed by inhabitant householders receiving neither alms nor poor relief. This group included Westminster, the borough constituency with the largest electorate: about 8,000 in the first half of the eighteenth century. In the twenty-seven corporation boroughs the right of voting was limited to the corporation; in the twenty-nine burgage boroughs to specific pieces of property; and in the six freeholder boroughs to those who owned freeholds.

These constituencies had smaller electorates than the householder, freeman, and scot and lot boroughs. Though the boroughs with smaller electorates did not all provide a picture of oligarchic control and corrupt practices, they were generally more stable in their politics and more amenable to outside influence than those with larger electorates. The diversity of the electoral system was not therefore restricted to the franchise. In addition, the seats with small electorates tended to have MPs who supported the government, increasingly so in the period of Old Corps Whiggery, while in that period those with larger electorates were more likely to vote for opposition candidates. While some settlements with very small populations were parliamentary boroughs, major towns, such as Birmingham, Chatham, Leeds, Manchester, Sheffield and Whitehaven, were not, though their voters could play a major role in county contests. Shifts in population did not lead to any redistribution of representation.

In Scotland there was also considerable variety in the franchise. In the county seats the right to vote belonged to freeholders possessing land valued at 40 shillings 'of old [medieval] extent', and to owners of land held of the Crown rated at £400 Scots. This restricted the electorate to men of landed substance, and in no county did the electorate exceed 200. In the Orkney and Shetland constituency there were no Shetland voters, as none of the Shetland landowners had applied for Scottish charters or a valuation of their holdings. Sutherland had a distinctive franchise, as the right to vote extended to those who were vassals of the Earl of Sutherland. The councils of Scottish burghs each elected a delegate and the delegates of each group of burghs then jointly elected an MP. Though Scottish constituencies required careful management, they tended to be a reliable source of support for the government. In Scottish counties with hereditary sheriffs, the sheriffs could return whomever they liked without consulting the freeholders, a measure stopped when hereditable sheriffdoms were abolished after the '45. The Welsh boroughs mirrored the English franchises, with corporation, freemen, and scot and lot electorates.[4] There was no secret ballot until 1872: voting was a public activity.

Socio-economic diversity was an element in the patchwork of local political worlds, while socio-economic issues, such as the canalisation of rivers, could play a major role in local politics. Such diversity and issues were matched in the political and religious spheres. Traditional political alignments, many of which drew on the still vital religious antagonisms of the previous two centuries, were important. In Scotland the division between Presbyterianism and Episcopalianism was crucial to society and politics, especially in the first half of the century. The former replaced the latter as the established Church there in 1689, episcopalian clergy being purged from their livings and from educational institutions.

The position of the various creeds differed in England, Scotland and Ireland, but, in general, legal codes tended to permit freedom of conscience and private worship, and limited or prohibited public worship, education and political power. In England few offices and professions were open to Dissenters (Protestant Nonconformists), and Catholics suffered particularly heavy restrictions, though practice could differ widely from legal position. The latter was not relaxed until the Catholic Relief Act of 1778, and it was not until 1791 that Catholics were allowed to hold their services legally. In reaction, as with so much of late seventeenth-century Britain, to the mid seventeenth-century crisis, an Anglican ascendancy had been established under Charles II. The Corporation Act (1661) and the first Test Act (1673) obliged members of borough corporations and office holders under the Crown to receive communion in the Church of England, and these remained in force throughout the eighteenth century. The Glorious Revolution loosened Anglican hegemony. Under the Act for Exempting their Majesties Protestant Subjects, Dissenting from the Church of England, from the Penalties of certain Laws, the concessionary but restrictive formulation of what is better known as the Toleration Act (1689), Dissenters who took the oaths of Supremacy and Allegiance and thirty-six of the thirty-nine Articles, and made the Declaration against Transubstantiation could obtain licences as ministers or schoolmasters, although these had to be registered with a bishop or at the Quarter Sessions. The Act was followed by the registration of numerous meeting-houses: twenty-three alone in Devon in 1689 and at least 113 in the county by the end of 1700.[5]

There were different tendencies within the Church of England and, in particular, a division between 'high' and latitudinarian clerics. The former were more hostile to other Protestant groups and more inclined to see a threat in toleration, a threat not only to religious orthodoxy, but also to the moral order and social cohesion that the Church was seen as sustaining. Dr Henry Sacheverell, an Anglican cleric and a Tory, felt able to argue in 1709 that the Church was in danger under the Revolution Settlement, as interpreted by Whigs. Four years later, George Parker, a Tory almanac writer, in his *Ephemeris* presented 'the cause of God' as confronted by the Whigs: 'the Faction working like moles under ground, in order to destroy our church and constitution'.[6] The Occasional Conformity (1711) and Schism (1714) Acts, designed respectively to prevent the circumvention of communion requirements for office-holding by Dissenters communicating once a year, and to make separate education for them illegal, measures both passed by Queen Anne's Tory ministry of 1710–14, were both repealed by the Whigs under George I in 1719. Nevertheless, attempts to repeal the Test and Corporation Acts failed.[7] The Whig party had traditionally been associated with Dissenters, but the cautious Whig administrations of Walpole and his successors were unwilling to tamper with religious fundamentals, not least because of the considerable groundswell of opinion in defence of the Church. Government control of ecclesiastical patronage brought the senior ranks of the Church of England closer to Whig governments. Though

Walpole obtained indemnity acts, protecting the Dissenters from malicious prosecution, each year bar 1730 and 1732, moves to repeal the Test and Corporation acts were defeated in 1736 and 1739, as they were again in 1787–90.[8] The strength of popular Anglicanism was demonstrated in 1753, when a vicious press campaign of anti-semitic hatred, with popular backing, forced the repeal of the Jewish Naturalisation Act of that year.[9]

If these events reaffirmed the identification of religion and state, in the form of government protection for the Church of England, they also both reflected and sustained local tensions. In much of Britain, hostility, or at least suspicion, between Anglicanism or Episcopalianism and Dissent or Presbyterianism, was a basic political axis,[10] and this would probably emerge more clearly were more regional studies to be carried out. Whether the Church was in danger or not at the national level, Anglicans felt it necessary to protect it in the localities, while, in the absence of a modern structure of party organisation, ecclesiastical links provided the basis of community and sociability that was so important in the development of political alignments. Religion was also a way to mobilise political passion and support (Doc. 6). The situation was complicated, however, by co-operation between Dissenters and Low Church Anglicans.

Ecclesiastical disputes were genuine disputes: this was a society in which disagreements about how best to worship God and seek salvation, how to organise the Church, and the relationship between Church and state, were matters of urgent concern, and the image of Hanoverian Britain as a 'polite' society is never more misleading than when it is taken to imply secularism or at least an absence of religious zeal. Instead, in Britain, as on the Continent, there is copious evidence both of massive observance of the formal requirements of the Churches and of widespread piety. Despite the claims of other Protestant groups, the established Churches were not devoid of energy, their congregations not sunk in torpor. These Churches ministered to their flocks and were not averse to religious campaigns, such as that waged in Wales in the early decades of the century by the Anglicans and the Dissenters, against Catholicism, drunkenness and profanity, and for salvation and literacy. The very nature of established Churches that sought to minister to all, in an age when religion was a social obligation as well as a personal spiritual experience, posed problems for some of those, both clergy and laity, who decried anything that might compromise the latter. Believers sure of their faith could find the compromises of national uniformity abhorrent. Dissatisfaction, however, reflected the importance of, and commitment to, religion, the churches and the clergy. Few believed that they could or should be dispensed with, or doubted the close relationships of faith and reason, church and state, clergy and laity, religion and the people. These relationships were not, however, untroubled. In the first half of the century, a Whiggish anticlericalism was still visible, as in the outcry against Edmund Gibson, labelled Dr Codex, for his attempts to revive the study and application of canon law. Jurisdictional and tithe disputes were also important. Alexander Horne, governor of the Isle of Man for its owner, the 10th Earl of Derby, had Thomas Wilson, Bishop of Sodor and Man, imprisoned in 1722 as a result of a dispute over ecclesiastical jurisdiction. The extent of popular religious observance and commitment is a matter of debate. The theme of the confessional state in Clark's *English Society* can be qualified by an appreciation that the position of the Church varied and that in some areas religious observance did not accord with expectations nor clerical conduct with duties. On the other hand, the Church was in a better state than that presented by Victorian critics. The Church of Ireland has recently been presented as catering adequately for its communicants and as well served by its clerics.[11]

Religious issues were therefore 'real' and worth fighting over, literally so as the riots against Dissenters in England in 1710, 1715 and 1791,[12] and against Catholics in Edinburgh and Glasgow in 1779 and in England in 1780.[13] indicated all too clearly. As a result of the riots in Scotland, the concessions given English Catholics by the 1778 Catholic Relief Act were not extended to north of the border. The Gordon Riots in London in 1780 arose from pressure for the repeal of the Act and were a challenge to order in the centre of empire that was greater than anything seen since the collapse of Charles I's authority in 1641–2. At the same time, religious antagonism to the Anglican world view of George III's government was one of the factors responsible for revolution in America.[14] Thus, though for different reasons, religion could be seen as playing a major role in the crisis of the British world at the beginning of the 1780s, a crisis that suggested that Britain, not France, was on the eve of major revolution.

Religious issues were also an expression or part of other disputes, ranging from that over the succession that followed the Glorious Revolution (Doc. 7), to the town–country tension that played a role in Anglican–Dissenter rivalries. Towns were often centres of Dissent, challenging Anglican religious-cultural hegemony just as they could seek to resist the attempts of the local gentry to control their parliamentary representation. Irrespective of religious issues, the question of independence from outside interests could play a major role in electoral contests (Doc. 8).

The role of local political divisions helps to explain the vitality of the local response to national issues. Far from there being a trickle-down system, in which the crucial debates and disputes occurred at the national level and those in the localities were simply a reflection, and then generally a limited one, a Greek chorus recording of crucial events happening off-stage, it is clear that there was a far more dynamic relationship and that the nature of politics needs to be reconceptualised. Instead of politics being a case of national and local, it was rather one of metropolitan (London, taken to include Whitehall and Westminster, neither of which was in the City of London) and local, and the two combined constituted national politics and indeed gave it its special character and energy. Precisely because the government tended to dominate Parliament and the Court, it was often in the localities (including the City of London), and in the means by which they were linked to the centres, that the principal political battles occurred. The dynamic nature of the relationship can be illustrated by considering the response of the major Midlands manufacturing town of Coventry to the Excise Crisis, the political storm that arose in 1733 over Sir Robert Walpole's proposal to extend the excise (taxation on goods, equivalent to modern VAT: Value Added Tax).[15] Coventry was dominated politically by the corporation (town council) which was controlled by Dissenters. They used their position to ensure that Whigs were elected to Parliament, though this was not always an easy process. A bitter contest in 1722 had led to the remark that Coventry 'has always been a mutinous election'.[16] The Excise Crisis was particularly serious because, under the Septennial Act, a general election had to be held at least once every seven years and, as the last had been held in 1727, one was therefore due in 1734 (Doc. 9). In

Ireland, in contrast, until the Octennial Act of 1768, the life of a Parliament was coterminous with that of the monarch so that after the general election of 1715 the next were not until 1727 and then 1760.

Opponents of the Excise throughout the country sought to stir up agitation against the government's proposals and to exert pressure on MPs. This caused difficulties for Sir Adolphus Oughton, one of Coventry's two MPs, a ministerial supporter with a constituency opposed to the Excise Scheme, and led him to abstain from the division on the bill on 14 March 1733 (Doc. 10). On 16 March 1733, however, Oughton was upset by his fellow Coventry MP, John Neale, speaking for the first time in the House of Commons, to which he had been elected in 1722. Neale declared that Coventry's instructions to its MPs against the Excise Bill were unrepresentative, and that 'he had had a letter from his Borough approving of the Scheme'. This put Oughton, who had been seeking the governorship of the British colony of Minorca, in a very difficult position (Doc. 11). Neale's claim led to a political storm in Coventry and a petition from the city to Parliament against the Excise bill, a development that exacerbated Oughton's difficulties by highlighting the competing pressures of constituency and ministry. Oughton did not present the petition; that was left to Neale, who had rapidly changed his position, and to William Bromley, Tory MP for Warwickshire; but he abstained in a division on 10 April despite being threatened with the loss of all promotion. Oughton did not receive the governorship of Minorca, but the loyalty that led to him voting in 1734 with the ministry against the repeal of the Septennial Act, in order to permit more frequent elections, an opposition objective, despite Coventry producing instructions in favour of a repeal, was rewarded when he was made a Brigadier-General in 1735.

Coventry was a sophisticated political environment, alert to issues both national and local, and its MPs could not rely on uncontested elections. Though Oughton and Neale were elected unopposed in 1727, Neale was defeated in 1734, only to be re-elected in a by-election in 1737. Similarly, Edward Southwell, opposition Whig MP for Bristol 1739–54, complained about criticisms from Bristol's electorate, 'if I am to suffer or to be run down for every single private vote in an affair where none but those who hear the arguments and pleadings can be judges, it is certain that no man can be more a slave than the representative of so populous a city'.[17]

It is easy when considering eighteenth-century parliamentary elections to stress corruption rather than issues, because the costs of elections were one of the major topics of electoral correspondence (Docs 12, 13 and 14). Many seats were not contested and there were a large number that were 'pocket boroughs', controlled or heavily influenced by patrons, most of whom, in the reigns of George I and George II, were Whigs. Thus, the 'Great Commoner', William Pitt the Elder, came into Parliament when he was elected unopposed for Old Sarum in 1735. This quintessential rotten borough returned two MPs, though it was entirely depopulated. Pitt's grandfather, Thomas 'Diamond' Pitt, who had made a fortune trading to India, had purchased the property that carried the right of election in 1691, and at the general election of 1734 William's elder brother was returned unopposed by the five voters for Old Sarum. As he had also been returned unopposed for Okehampton, where he owned much property, Thomas brought his brother in for Old Sarum. William sat for that seat until 1747, then for pocket boroughs of the Duke of Newcastle. In December 1756 he was elected for Okehampton and for the pocket borough of his Grenville in-laws at Buckingham, and in 1757 he transferred to Bath, which he had been invited to represent by the corporation, which enjoyed a monopoly of the franchise. Only one of his elections, Seaford in 1747, was contested. In addition, government influence in certain boroughs was sufficient to get some of its nominees elected.

It is easy to understand why Charles Delafaye, an Under-Secretary of State, felt able to write in 1733 about the forthcoming general election, 'he that gives more money and most wine will be chosen'.[18] Tancred Robinson wrote of his election campaign for York in 1722 against Edward Thompson, 'who fell to open bribery in the streets'. Mary Caesar, wife of the Tory MP for Hertfordshire, claimed that the Excise bill forced the ministry to spend massive sums in the 1734 general election, 'A vast expense attended the Court in making good their elections, it having raised such a fire in the counties against the voters for it, that only money could squench'.[19] Complaints about corruption were not, however, restricted to opposition spokesmen, who tended to lack the resources of the ministry. Contested elections were expensive for most candidates. It is not therefore surprising that Henry Ibbetson and William Thornton offered to stand for York in 1747 against the Tory MPs, provided that the Whig gentry in the county agreed to subscribe to their expenses. Ibbetson also asked the ministry for £2,000. There was little response from the county Whigs, possibly because the decision had been taken to accept a compromise over the county representation, and because they harboured bitter memories of the expensive subscription campaign that had failed to reverse the opposition victory in the 1734 county election by a parliamentary petition. Fearing the financial troubles that the ministerial victor in 1741, Edward Thompson, had suffered, Ibbetson withdrew from the contest. One of the Tories did likewise, and thus there was an uncontested election. Several contested elections were notoriously expensive. This was true of Oxfordshire in 1754, Northampton in 1768, and Westminster in 1788. The Northampton contest arose from an attempt by Earl Spencer to break the influence of two other county peers, the Earls of Northampton and Halifax. The expense helped to bankrupt the two latter: 'The public houses were open for two or three days during the canvass, and in that short space of time £1,600 was spent on each side.' One commentator, referring to the legal obligation on MPs to own a certain amount of landed property, wrote 'the Masters of Public Houses etc will have all the Estates, and the Members not left with a Qualification'. After 1754 there was no Oxfordshire contest until 1826.[20]

Finance and detailed calculations about the personal interests of constituents (Doc. 15) thus seem to have been crucial. This could lead to a situation in which consultation and representation, let alone any element of democracy, might seem to be absent. The ability of estate stewards to organise the votes of tenants and thus to make 'it possible for the governing élite to adjust to the changed political circumstances' after the Glorious Revolution 'without chaos or public violence' has recently been emphasised. Many elections were unopposed, while some quite populous boroughs were under the electoral control of particular, often non-resident, families. Such control commonly reflected local property, though it was generally a relationship that had to be kept alive by careful management, as much as by expenditure.

Charles Rose Ellis recalled to Thomas, 2nd Earl of Chichester, how in 1794 the latter had asked him 'to undertake the re-establishment of your interest, arising out of family property in and near to the borough [Seaford], by purchasing several houses then on sale'.[21] The Ryders controlled one of the Tiverton seats from 1734 to the Great Reform Act of 1832, though their interest had to be managed with care.[22] Irrespective of any urban property, local aristocrats and gentry could be of considerable consequence in controlling or influencing borough representation. One of the Winchester seats was contested between two local magnates, the Dukes of Bolton and Chandos. In 1784 Chandos, who owned the nearby Avington estate, brought in his brother-in-law Richard Gamon, who was to sit until 1812, displacing Henry Flood, whom he had elected the previous year, without giving much attention to the views of the electors.[23] This was scarcely surprising. In the thirty-five years after the Winchester by-election of 1751, there were six general and three by-elections there, not a single one of which was contested.

Electoral corruption might seem to be linked to corruption at the political centre, to a world in which ideas were subordinated to self-interest (Doc. 16). And yet, it is necessary to be cautious on both heads, to note the role of issues and political independence (Doc. 17) and the extent to which corrupt practices can be seen in part as means by which politics continued in a world in which ideology and conviction played a major role.

This was true at both the national and the local level. Patronage and political management alone were insufficient to keep governments in power.[24] Just as there were limits to the deference of voters towards their social superiors, more especially landlords,[25] so also the effectiveness of parliamentary management should not be exaggerated. Policies were also important (Doc. 18). Walpole devised a political programme of peace, low taxation, no further favours for the Dissenters and no extension of governmental power into the localities, which was followed by Henry Pelham, First Lord of the Treasury 1743–54, and helped to produce parliamentary and ministerial stability for most of the period 1721–54. It is significant that the patronage resources at the disposal of the government could not prevent serious political crises and defeats when the ministry took initiatives that failed to carry political opinion with them: over the Excise and the Jewish Naturalisation Act. It is also noteworthy that when the Walpolean prescription was abandoned, political difficulties increased. War with Spain (1739–48) and France (actual hostilities, 1743–8, 1754–63) played a major role in the political crises leading to the falls of Walpole (1742), Carteret (1744) and Newcastle (1756).

At the local level, the independence of the electorate can emerge clearly, as can the role of issues. The two were sometimes combined in a preference for local men. Independence from interests deemed outside was seen as a crucial issue in what was often an intensely local political world. This world was more open, particularly through the press, to outside views, than ever before, but still saw them through a local prism. In 1718 John Clavering, a Whig from an old county Durham family, had proposed himself as a candidate for Newcastle and wrote to his relative Lady Cowper that his decision was not 'unacceptable to many here, most people desiring to have one of their country [i.e. county or region] for this representative, before a stranger as Wrightson is'. William Wrightson MP, a Tory Yorkshireman, had married into a wealthy Newcastle merchant family, but was clearly regarded as a stranger by some, and he was to be defeated in 1722 by William Carr, a prominent Whig Newcastle merchant. As so often, the precise relationship between national political alignments and a sense of local identity is unclear. The same year, William Stanhope, MP for Derby since 1715, complained that he was not going to be re-elected there, 'where I thought it was impossible for me to meet with any opposition . . . when out of sight . . . all services forgotten, for certainly I did for that town the greatest they had to wish for, by making their river navigable'.[26] Despite the usual dominance in the town of the Cavendishes, Dukes of Devonshire, and the Stanhopes, Earls of Chesterfield, Stanhope, Ambassador to Spain, was unable to defend his interest. The Cavendish–Stanhope interest regained its dominance in 1727 in what was a borough with a large electorate (about 700 freemen), winning uncontested elections in 1727, 1734, 1736, 1741, 1746 and 1748 and contested ones in 1734, 1742 and 1747, but in a 1748 by-election, a townsman, Thomas Rivett, defeated Thomas Stanhope in a determined effort to display local independence, of which the 1722 result may have been a precursor. Rivett tricked the Duke of Devonshire, whose electoral agent he was, by using Devonshire's interest to get himself returned.

Elected for the populous and politically-aware seat of Bristol in 1774, Burke argued to his constituents that an MP should be guided by 'the general good . . . He owes you, not his industry only, but his judgment; and he betrays you, not serves you, if he sacrifices it to your opinion.' Burke's neglect, however, of 'local prejudices', in the shape of Bristol's negative views on proposals of freer trade for Ireland, helped him to come bottom of the poll in 1780.[27]

Election propaganda could stress the local dimension. Whig propaganda in York in 1747 emphasised the importance of representatives 'born and bred amongst us'. The *Daily Courant* of 18 May 1734 stressed local issues in its report on the uncontested re-election of a member of an old-established local family, Edward Thompson MP, at York: 'The company of substantial and loyal citizens that went with Mr. Thompson, wore orange-coloured cockades, and carried a flag with the motto Navigation, in memory of his great service in obtaining a bill for the improvement of their river, hallowed, Thompson, Liberty and Navigation'. The colour of the cockades was a reference to William III, an echo of the Whig attempt to identify the party with national interests in the shape of the Revolution Settlement.

Thompson's election propaganda was a powerful reminder of the role of MPs in forwarding local legislation at Westminster, one of the most important links between localities and national institutions.[28] The sense of locality that continued to play a role in elections was therefore not without political meaning. The Lewes election of 1768 showed the importance both of powerful political interests *and* of local feeling. Lewes was a constituency where the local magnate, the Duke of Newcastle, from his nearby seats of Halland and Bishopstone, had considerable influence and his support for Thomas Hampden was very important in the latter's election (Doc. 19). Hampden's father was the 1st Viscount Hampden and his uncle was Richard Trevor, Bishop of Durham, and a close friend of Newcastle. Thomas Hampden satisfied the requirements of local patronage, but there was unease about an outsider, William Plumer, a Hertfordshire gentleman, who had been put up for Lewes successfully by Newcastle in the uncontested 1763 by-election (Doc. 20). Plumer was approved as candidate for Lewes by a general meeting, but, in the event, he preferred to stand for Hertfordshire, where he was elected without opposition. Clearly it was necessary in the management of Lewes to take note of local political sensitivity, and this helped to lead to the election, alongside Hampden, of Thomas Hay, a local man whom Newcastle was unwillingly obliged to accept.

MPs were expected to take note of the interests of their constituents, and this constrained the responses of MPs who saw themselves as independents. In 1748 John, Viscount Perceval was 'pestered with petitions from persons in and about Weobley'.[29] These interests were not confined to matters of patronage, or, rather, patronage should not be interpreted in a narrow sense. Politics in the localities was also about issues. The Yorkshire election in the 1741 general election had been unopposed, the country representation being gained by Viscount Morpeth, an opposition Whig, and Sir Miles Stapylton, a Tory. Morpeth shortly afterwards died of venereal disease and his seat was contested by George Fox, a Tory, and Cholmley Turner, a ministerial Whig and former MP for the county. Turner was induced to submit himself to 'the command of the gentlemen', as expressed by his unanimous adoption at a general Whig county meeting. There is no doubt that the Yorkshire election was fought on party lines, as is clear both from the surviving political correspondence and electoral propaganda. The leading county newspaper, the *York Courant*, in its issue of 20 October 1741, carried a letter from J. S. of Leeds attacking Turner's support for ministerial measures, including the Convention of the Pardo, the ministry's attempt to settle Anglo-Spanish differences, his support for the Septennial Act, a standing (permanent) army, and government fiscal demands. A week later, friends of Turner's replied, claiming that the opposition was using the Convention as 'a cant word, adopted without meaning, and echo'd out amongst the people to inflame and abuse them'. Fox was unsuccessful. On 21 January 1742 Turner was elected to the largest constituency in the country. Turner's vote (8005–7049) was higher than those he had polled in 1727 and 1734, suggesting that support for the ministerial Whig candidate was buoyant less than a fortnight before Walpole had decided that he would have to resign (Doc. 21).

National issues were translated to the local scale and vice

versa. Electioneering in Sussex during a controversy over the conduct of the war with Spain, Lord Abergavenny noted in 1740, 'the people here ask a great many questions about fleets, marines, etc. etc. which are too many to be particularised, and too hard for me to answer'.[30] That summer the charge to the Essex Grand Jury was designed to explain and defend government policy. The judge 'spoke very honourably of the Convention [with Spain] and of all the King's measures, first for preserving the peace, and since, for carrying on the war, with vigour and success'.[31] In Weymouth opposition to Walpole was bound up in disputes over the town's charter. John Tucker, one of the MPs, took great care to keep his constituents informed (Doc. 22). Such activities were part of what was simultaneously the maintenance of political links between centre and locality and a process of politicisation or deepening of a national political consciousness. It is instructive to compare two speeches made by Dorset MPs in 1761 and 1789. At the electoral meeting held at The Crown in Blandford Forum on 13 January 1761 to introduce the candidates for the county at the forthcoming uncontested general election the politicians said little of policy and the surviving account is a manuscript one (Doc. 23). Twenty-eight years later, a meeting held at Dorchester to pass an Address of Thanks to William Pitt, for his conduct in the Regency Crisis, was reported at some length in the press. The politicised nature of the occasion and the extent to which the Dorset MPs were divided were clear (Doc. 24). Charles Sturt, like his father, stressed his independency, but the changing nature of the political world, the sharper awareness of politics and politicians, were indicated by the appearance of a reasonably lengthy account of his speech in print. In addition, it has been argued that the controversy over war with America led people to stress their perception of a fundamental unity between local and national political structures and alignments.[32]

It would be a mistake to see a development of national political connections and consciousness in linear terms. The religious changes of 1530–1665 had led to repeated centrally-directed local changes and no eighteenth-century government acted in as intrusive a fashion as Henry VIII's had done with the Dissolution of the Monasteries or Cromwell with the rule of the Major-Generals. Yet, agencies for representing local views and articulating a national political debate had been weak in the sixteenth and seventeenth centuries, not least because for long periods Parliament did not meet. The shift, as a result of the Revolution Settlement, to annual sessions of a Parliament elected at least at regular intervals (though not in Ireland), and with defined powers therefore made possible a major change in the political culture. Parliament was important not so much as a forum where government could be defeated, a relatively rare occurrence in the eighteenth century, but as one that encouraged a change in the nature of political debate, by creating a regular agency for publicly representing political views.

Notes

1   F. O'Gorman, *Voters, Patrons and Parties: the unreformed electorate of Hanoverian England, 1734–1832* (Oxford, 1989).

2   D. Rollison, *The Local Origins of Modern Society: Gloucestershire 1500–1800* (1992); P. Hudson ed., *Regions and Industries: a perspective on the Industrial Revolution in Britain* (Cambridge, 1989).

3   S. W. Baskerville and P. Adman, 'The socio-economic context of voter behaviour in Cheshire elections, 1681–1734', ESRC Award 231988 report; Langford, *Polite and Commercial*, p. 718.

4   Namier and Brooke, *The House of Commons 1754–1790* (3 vols, 1964) i, 2–46. A different classification of borough constituencies can be found in O'Gorman, *Voters*: venal, proprietorial, corporation, patronage, open; Holmes, *The Electorate and the National Will in the First Age of Party* (Lancaster, 1976), pp. 28–9.

5   O. P. Grell, Israel and N. Tyacke eds., *From Persecution to Toleration: the Glorious Revolution and religion in England* (Oxford, 1991); E. Duffy, *Peter and Jack: Roman Catholics and Dissent in eighteenth century England* (1982); A. Warne, *Church and society in eighteenth-century Devon* (Newton Abbot, 1969), pp. 92–3.

6   G. Holmes, *The Trial of Doctor Sacheverell* (1973).

7   G. Townend, 'Religious radicalism and conservatism in the Whig Party under George I: the repeal of the Occasional Conformity and Schism Acts', *Parliamentary History*, VII (1988), pp. 24–44.

8   G. M. Ditchfield, 'The parliamentary struggle over the repeal of the Test and Corporation Acts, 1787–1790', *English Historical Review*, LXXXIX (1974), pp. 551–77.

9   T. W. Perry, *Public Opinion, Propaganda, and Politics in Eighteenth-Century England: a study of the Jew Bill of 1753* (Cambridge, Mass., 1962).

10   A. N. Newman, 'Elections in Kent and its parliamentary rep-

resentation 1715–54' (unpublished D. Phil., Oxford, 1957), pp. 35–6; DeKrey, *Fractured Society*, pp. 74–120; J. Barry, 'The press and the politics of culture in Bristol 1660–1775', in Black and Gregory eds., *Culture, Politics and Society*, p. 52.

11   P. Virgin, *The Church in an Age of Negligence* (Cambridge, 1989); J. R. Guy ed., *The Diocese of Llandaff in 1763, The primary visitation of Bishop Ewer* (Cardiff, 1991); W. Gibson, *Religion and Society 1760–1850* (1993); Connolly, *Religion, Law, and Power*.

12   Rogers, 'Riot and popular Jacobitism in early Hanoverian England', in Cruickshanks ed., *Ideology and Conspiracy*, pp. 70–88; Monod, *Jacobitism and the English People 1688–1788*, pp. 161–232.

13   C. Haydon, 'The Gordon riots in the English provinces', *Historical Research*, LXIII (1990), pp. 354–9, and *Anti-Catholicism in Eighteenth-Century England* (Manchester, 1993).

14   Clark, *The Language of Liberty: political discourse and social dynamics in the Anglo-American World, 1660–1800* (Cambridge, 1994).

15   Langford, *The Excise Crisis* (Oxford, 1975).

16   George Tilson, Under-Secretary of State, to Charles Whitworth, envoy in Berlin, 13 April 1722, BL. Add. 37388 fo. 301.

17   Southwell to —, 15 February 1742, Bristol, City Library, Southwell papers vol. 7.

18   Delafaye to Earl Waldegrave, 2 March 1733, Chewton House, Chewton Mendip, papers of James, Earl Waldegrave.

19   Leeds, City Archives Office, Newby Hall papers 2501; J. F. Quinn, 'York elections in the age of Walpole', *Northern History*, XXII (1986); BL. Add. 62558 fo. 49.

20   Lord North to Earl of Guildford, 14 October, J. Osborn to Guildford, 8 October 1767, Bod. Ms. North Adds c 4 fos 102, 106; D. Spinney, *Rodney* (1969), pp. 226–37.

21   D. R. Hainsworth, *Stewards, Lords and People: the estate steward and his world in later Stuart England* (Cambridge, 1992), p. 158; Ellis to Chichester, 24 December 1812, Lewes, East Sussex RO. AMS 6005 no. 23.

22   J. Bourne, *Georgian Tiverton: the political memoranda of Beavis Wood 1768–98* (Devon and Cornwall Record Society, new series, XXIX, 1986).

23   W. J. Petchey, *A Prospect of Maldon 1500–1689* (Chelmsford, 1991), p. 252; Flood to Chandos, 10, 15, 23, 27 April 1784, Huntington Library, Stowe Collection 10 fos 47–51.

24   Black, *Walpole*, pp. 23–88.

25   Landau, 'Independence, deference, and voter participation: the behaviour of the electorate in early-eighteenth-century Kent', *Historical*

Journal, XXII (1979), pp. 561–83; Clark, *English Society*, pp. 15–26; Baskerville, Adman and K. F. Beedham, 'Manuscript poll books and English county elections in the first age of party', *Archives*, 19 (October 1991), pp. 400–1.

26   Hertford, Hertfordshire CRO. D/EP F196 fo. 64; Stanhope to Sir Luke Schaub, 27 April 1722, New York, Public Library, Hardwicke Collection vol. 59.

27   P. T. Underdown, 'Edmund Burke, the commissary of his Bristol constituents', *English Historical Review* LXXIII (1958), pp. 252–69.

28   S. Handley, 'Local legislative initiatives for economic and social development in Lancashire, 1689–1731', *Parliamentary History*, IX (1990), pp. 14–37.

29   J. V. Beckett, 'A back-bench MP in the eighteenth century: Sir James Lowther of Whitehaven', *Parliamentary History*, 1 (1982), p. 94; J. Green to Perceval, 17 November 1748, BL. Add. 47012B fol. 150.

30   Abergavenny to Newcastle, 13 July 1740, BL. Add. 32693 fo. 485.

31   Colonel Martin Bladen MP to Newcastle, 17 July 1740, BL. Add. 32694 fos 165–6.

32   J. E. Bradley, *Popular Politics and the American Revolution in England: petitions, the Crown, and public opinion* (Macon, Georgia, 1986), p. 11.

4

Parliament

The Westminster Parliament was a great success in the eighteenth century. It passed a growing quantity of legislation, a testimony to its importance in the political system. In addition, the Westminster Parliament became the British Parliament, the sole Parliament in the British Isles as a result of the Acts of Union with Scotland (1707) and Ireland (1800). The role of Parliament appeared especially important to Continental visitors, for only in Sweden, Poland and the United Provinces (Netherlands) were there comparable institutions and none was so successful: the Swedish Age of Liberty came to an end in 1772, while the Dutch Estates General and the Polish Diet were proverbial for delay and disagreement. Their systems of government were also discredited, the Dutch by the political breakdown and civil conflict of 1786–7, the Polish by the failures leading to the three partitions of the country. The British system, in contrast, could be presented as excellent, an excellence that reflected the balanced nature of the constitution and that was demonstrated by the successes of Britain: in avoiding autocracy at home, in imperial struggle with France in the Seven Years War, in the British revival from the disaster of the American War of Independence (Doc. 25).

Parliament, or rather the House of Commons,[1] for the Lords has been generally neglected,[2] has dominated the discussion of eighteenth-century politics and been central to analyses both of the structure of politics and of the impact of particular controversies. If over the last two decades, more work has been devoted to an alternative structure of politics, to the world of popular urban activity, this has not displaced attention from Parliament and has indeed in part been seen as important in so far as it affected parliamentary conduct.

And yet the significance of parliamentary discussion of policy can be qualified, while it can be suggested that any assessment of Parliament's role requires a more specific approach, one that is more sensitive to particular issues and years. Parliament can be seen as a sphere of political activity, a means for other agencies to pursue their interests and views, as much as an autonomous force. The qualification of Parliament's importance has various sources. It is but part of the more general realisation that the tendency to stress public spheres of discussion can be misleading. They were less commonly spheres of decision-making, or sources of the decisions that were taken, than is usually appreciated. There is, however, a marked reluctance to accept this situation or to consider its consequences. Instead, there is a powerful sense that the public sphere, Parliament, the culture of print, the world of campaigns, agitation, propaganda and public opinion, must somehow have been not solely important, but instead central to the processes of decision-making. It would be foolish to deny the importance of the sphere, but, equally, the stress on the public sphere advanced by some scholars can rather be described as an act of faith than as an assessment based on an understanding of the steps by which decisions were usually taken. By concentrating on crises in which public manifestations of opposition to the government were notable, it is possible to present a misleading view of the difficulties that ministries encountered, one that concentrates on the relationship between policy and public, especially popular, opposition. As the crises are automatically defined by the strength of the latter, an impression is created that the central political problem was that of defending policy in such contexts, and that the political chronology of the period can be readily traced from crisis to crisis. A 'structure of politics' has been advanced for this public opposition, one based on urban institutions, sociability and manifestations: clubs, petitions, newspapers, instructions and addresses. In addition, an ideology has been discerned, one of 'closely intertwined . . . Patriotism, nationalism, and commercial expansion', which 'continued to resonate into the 1750s',[3] and became of

75

greater importance thereafter. The political context of this ideology altered, however, so that in the 1790s these concepts were loyalist, rather than oppositional in their direction.

To consider government policy without paying attention to the range, intensity and impact of public debate would be foolish. An ability to profit from or manipulate extra-parliamentary public pressures could be crucial politically (Doc. 27), but their impact has been exaggerated, not least in terms of their role in defining a chronology of crisis, an agenda of study. Thus, the period 1730–70 becomes a matter of the Excise Crisis of 1733, followed by the Jenkins's Ear agitation of 1738–9,[4] the anti-Hanoverian upsurge of 1742–4, the Pittite onslaught on Newcastle in 1754–6 and then, from 1763, the Wilkite controversy.[5] Other episodes can of course have their place: the support for Admiral Vernon in 1739–42, the agitation against Jewish Naturalisation in 1753 (Doc. 26),[6] or that against the cider excise in 1763–6.[7] This is, however, as misleading as studying the Middle Ages by proceeding from the Norman Conquest to the Wars of the Roses via the civil war in Stephen's reign, Magna Charta, Simon de Montfort, Edward II and Richard II, with Parliament being seen as arising from these confrontations. Clearly comparisons and links between eighteenth-century crises can be discerned, and this has been done in order to demonstrate a degree of consistency and coherence that is seen as an important aspect of the significance of the agitation discussed. One recent study claims that the Vernon agitation

> demonstrates the growing importance of Britain's empire in the nascent political and national consciousness of ordinary citizens. As the grievances of a portion of Britain's overseas trading community began to receive national attention, mercantile interests and opposition ideology converged to define 'liberty and property' in terms antithetical to the domestic and foreign policies of the Walpolean state. In doing so, the final stage of the opposition to Walpole adumbrated many of the issues of the Seven Years War, stimulating the articulation of a popular mercantilist vision of empire as the sole means to national greatness.[8]

Whatever degree of consistency and coherence can be found in the arguments advanced in this public debate, their direct political consequence, however, was far more episodic. Furthermore, a concentration on them can create, as it possibly reflects, a misleading impression of the principal political problems facing ministries in the field of policy, one that minimises the impact of dissension within governments.

This approach leads to a misunderstanding of the role of Parliament, and to its presentation largely in terms of a forum for the advancement or rejection of public aspirations, a sphere in short for the conduct of public politics. This was clearly of consequence, but its role has been exaggerated, for, by focusing on the debate between government and opposition, and then largely in terms of this as an aspect of a wider struggle between antithetical values and 'consciousnesses', the importance of Parliament in three fields is minimised. First, it is important to note the passage of private and local Acts, which took up much parliamentary time and reflected the often very specific importance of parliamentary legislation. The number of private bills passed by the Commons rose from 68 in 1760 to 210 in 1800. Second, there was general legislation that was not controversial in party political terms. This was true, for example, of proposals concerned with social policy, such as the reform of the Poor Law, the financing of workhouses, the punishment of crime, bills against blasphemy and duelling, and the treatment of debtors.[9] Such legislation reflected the 'reactive' nature of much government, for much was undertaken not by ministerial initiative, but as the result of back-bench moves or pressure from lobby groups, such as the Society for Promoting Christian Knowledge.[10] Thus the importance of public opinion for Parliament was not restricted to elections. Parliamentary views were, in part, a reflection of continual pressure from outside Westminster, through personal contacts, pressure groups and the press.

Third, the importance of Parliament to discussion and contention within government has been underrated or more commonly neglected. And yet, its role in this field was of major significance. For, prior to the death of George II in 1760, the major fault line in the struggle over foreign policy, and related matters, such as the size of the armed forces, which were the crucial political issues in 1717–18 and for most of the 1740s and 1750s, lay not between government and people, however defined and represented, with Parliament managed by the former but open to the arguments of the latter, but rather within the government and centring on the apparent needs created by the Hanoverian commitment. In 1760 the situation altered. Hanover was displaced, but not due to any triumph by extra-parliamentary forces or by widely-held Patriot attitudes. Instead the change reflected a marked shift in the dynastic dynamic, away from the Anglo-Hanoverian monarchy of George I and George II and towards a more clearly British conception on the part of the new king.[11]

Under George II it is clear that parliamentary attitudes and the real and alleged problems of managing the Commons played a major role in discussions over policy within the government. These problems reflected in part what might appear to be the less clear-cut nature of party allegiances in the period, but what instead could be presented as a consequence of the divided nature of the Whig inheritance. Whereas the division between Whigs and Tories was in the majority of cases readily apparent, that between ministerial and opposition Whigs was porous, a situation demonstrated when Walpole fell in 1742 and again in the struggles over the position of Carteret, Pitt and other Whigs in 1744–6. It is not surprising therefore that in some moments of crisis governmental majorities fell, in part owing to defections of MPs to the opposition, but more generally owing to a rise in the number of abstentions. The latter had been crucial in Walpole's two major parliamentary defeats, the enforced withdrawal of the excise legislation in 1733 and his loss of control in the Commons in the winter of 1741–2. Once the parliamentary majority of a ministry began to fall and rumours circulated of government changes, it proved very difficult to retain the loyalty of Whig MPs keen to make bargains with those they believed were about to take power, who were bound to be prominent Whigs. In February 1735, when the ministerial majority fell to 53 in a Commons division over increasing the size of the army, the Earl of Egmont noted in his diary, 'I hear the Court is not pleased at seeing so small a majority, and on this occasion, Mons. Chavigny, the French Ambassador, told my son what the late Lord Sunderland once told him, namely, that whenever an English Minister had but 60 majority in the House of Commons he was undone'. Various statements were attributed to Walpole to the effect that if the majority fell below 40 or 50 his power was lost. When on 9 December 1741 Walpole's majority dramatically dropped to 7 in a division in which 439 MPs voted, Newcastle observed, 'it was occasioned by the absence of friends'. The same cause was blamed for defeats later in the month.[12]

Thus, however the party alignments were defined, ministerial majorities were uncertain; victory in elections and the subsequent opening of the bazaar of patronage to parliamentarians did not necessarily entail either quiescent sessions or, more seriously, stable majorities. Far from Parliament being part of a corrupt but stable *ancien régime*, which could only be swayed, and eventually overthrown, by outside pressure and mass politicisation, Parliament was instead an integral part of a political system that was open to debate and far from inflexible over policy.

It was not therefore surprising that the management of Parliament was seen as a central task of government and that it bore directly on differences over policy and place within ministries. In general concern over management led to two different and sometimes clashing themes in the field of foreign policy: a stress on a clear-cut defence of what were seen as national interests and a wish to restrain expenditure. These could coincide, as in the reluctance to support subsidies to foreign powers, but also clashed, as in 1739 when concern about the parliamentary response to the continuing crisis with Spain took precedence over anxiety about financial considerations. In 1739 there was dissension over the best policy to follow for domestic reasons, the Duke of Newcastle arguing that it was essential to adopt a more aggressive attitude towards Spain, while Walpole strove to maintain his more cautious policy. Walpole lost, Britain went to war and thereafter greater priority was placed on policies designed to achieve success in the struggle with first Spain and later France. This, however, created problems between on the one hand military and diplomatic priorities and problems and on the other hand domestic expectations. In part this was an aspect of the struggle between government and opposition (Doc. 28).

It would be misleading, however, to see the formal struggle between government and opposition as the only, or even necessarily the most important, aspect both of political discussion and contention in Parliament, and therefore of ministerial concern about the parliamentary consequences of government policy. This question is linked to the issue of the cohesion of political groups, the strength of the party system. A two-party, Whig–

Tory, alignment has been seen as central to the politics of Anne's reign.[13] Such an examination is supported by an analysis of division lists of parliamentary votes, but a concentration on this formal, public aspect of parliamentary activity, debates and votes may underrate dissension within the somewhat amorphous parties. Thus, the Tory ministry of 1710–14 faced serious divisions over the succession, with a large parliamentary Jacobite group requiring careful management.[14] The Whigs gained office in 1714 and won the election of 1715 which was fought as a Whig–Tory contest, but in 1717–20 the Whigs split over the pursuit of place and foreign policy differences, Walpole leading the opposition to the ministry of James, 1st Viscount Stanhope and Charles, 3rd Earl of Sunderland.[15]

There were Whig splits again, both in the early 1720s and then from 1725 on, but a certain political coherence was produced by Walpole's shaping of the ministerial Whigs into a strong governing party. George II's decision, after initial hesitation when he came to the throne in 1727, to keep Walpole as first minister was important to this process of consolidation. Whigs who opposed the government sought at least tactical understandings with the Tories. Some politicians sought to take this further. In 1722 Archibald Hutcheson, a Tory, sought 'to persuade honest Whigs and Tories to unite against the common enemies of the liberties of the Kingdom'. This process was given greater force from the mid-1720s by the combined efforts of the maverick Tory Henry St John, Viscount Bolingbroke and the disappointed Whig William Pulteney. A ministerial pamphleteer of 1727 noted the partial success of this attempt to create a new configuration when he commented that Tory language 'is of late very frequently in the mouths of a quite different set of people'.[16] The new 'Country' alignment failed, however, to triumph in either Parliament or elections, and Walpole survived the political crisis of 1733, the Excise controversy and the associated attempt to dislodge him at Court. Mary Caesar, the wife of a Jacobite who had lost his seat at the 1734 election, reflected on the Excise, 'like unto a flash of lightning the spirit of the people came and went'.[17]

The political situation altered as the alignments of the late 1730s fractured under the strain of the new political world that emerged as a consequence of the growing difficulties that

Walpole confronted in 1740–2 and, specifically, as a result first of the general election in 1741 and secondly of the manoeuvres associated with the fall of Walpole. Between Walpole's resignation in February 1742 and the reconstitution of a relatively united ministry which was securely in control of Parliament, a process that was not complete until the spring of 1746,[18] political alignments were recognisably different from the position in the late 1730s. In some respects the essential political situation was unchanged. The political world was divided between government and opposition, the ministry composed of Whigs who supported the Protestant succession, the opposition divided between opposition Whigs who similarly backed the Hanoverian dynasty, and Tories whose dynastic loyalty was more uncertain and whose relations with the opposition Whigs was fraught with suspicion.

However, despite this structural continuity, there were essential differences in the situation after the fall of Walpole. The composition and policy of the ministry, the identity of government and opposition Whigs, were unsettled and the political world not only was volatile, but also was seen as such. It is not surprising that Whig politicians, both individuals and groups, manoeuvred to gain advantage, nor that there was a significant debate amongst the Whigs as to what government policies should be. This was a debate in which the Tories took little role, and it was one that subsided after the consolidation of the Pelhamite regime in early 1746, which explains in part the nature and chronology of the debate.

During these years the debate over policy was especially bitter, a product in part of the complex and difficult international situation, but even more of the need for political definition and the opportunities for political advancement and advantage in Britain. The divisions *within* the government, especially that between Carteret and the Pelhams (the Duke of Newcastle and his brother, Henry Pelham) who had been on opposite sides politically in 1730–42, interacted with the debate between ministry and opposition to an extent that had not existed in the late 1730s, and thus the parliamentary aspect of this debate can be understood, and commonly had most political importance, as an aspect of the related struggles for predominance and over policy within the ministry. The arguments of the parliamentary critics of Carteret took on meaning and weight as part of a wider debate amongst the Whigs. The opposition Whig speakers in the debate on the address on 1 December 1743, such as Pitt and George Dodington, made statements that dramatised the views of *ministerial* opponents of Carteret. Pitt declared 'That the Parliament never engaged but in a defensive war for the house of Austria not in a war of equivalent, not in a war of indemnification . . . that minister, who seems to have renounced the British Nation. I can never approve of a war of which neither the end or the means have yet been ascertained'.[19] A year later Dodington was appointed to the lucrative post of Treasurer of the Navy, while Pitt joined the ministry in the spring of 1746, both men beneficiaries of the defeat of Carteret. This theme of the role of the parliamentary debate as taking on significance as part of the struggle within the ministry can be extended, though the relationship is not easy to assess, in part because, in a political society in which politicians were in close contact, the need to commit ideas to paper was limited. This was encouraged by suspicions of interception arising from governmental control of the postal system. Considerations of parliamentary management played a major role in ministerial discussions about the desirability of peace and about acceptable terms in the winter of 1747–8. They were also important in the debate in 1748–54 between Newcastle and his colleagues about the desirability of a costly, interventionist diplomacy. Parliamentary management was obviously a crucial factor in the political crisis of 1754–7, but Newcastle's resignation in 1756 despite the size of his majority indicated that the matter was not simply one of parliamentary arithmetic. A government needed a reliable manager in the Commons, but there were obvious problems if the ministry was divided or otherwise unable to provide the manager with the firm support he required, factors that helped to account for the difficulties of management in 1717–20, 1754–7 and 1763–7.[20] A divided ministry and a weak manager encouraged attack from politicians who hoped to join and otherwise alter the government, not to overthrow it, although such politicians were quite willing to turn for support to those who sought more substantial changes. Conversely if the ministry was united, then criticism, whether parliamentary or extra-parliamentary, of its policy was of slight consequence, as the critics of the Pitt–Newcastle administration (1757–61) came to appreciate and as Pitt himself discovered when he attacked the terms of the Peace of Paris in 1762–3 without success; although, in both cases, it is also necessary to assess the consequences of widespread support for governmental policy.[21]

Parliament was therefore politically most important for much of the period not as a forum in which a ministry could be overthrown, but rather as one that could affect and reflect political battles being waged inside the ministry, and more generally within the political élite. In these struggles a parliamentary perspective, an emphasis on the need to manage Parliament, could be advanced for tactical political reasons, rather than as an objective assessment of the views of parliamentarians or the exigencies of parliamentary management. This was certainly to be the case with the rise of Pitt. In late 1745 George II argued that the defeat of opposition motions indicated that Pitt's support for the ministry was unnecessary, and the same appeared true in late 1754 and again in the winter of 1755–6. This did not prevent Pitt's rise to office. Aside from the fact that political and parliamentary confidence were not measurable by objective criteria, not simply a matter of the size of majorities, and that this was especially the case in periods of crisis, the resort to the issue of parliamentary management in order to advance particular political goals was tactically valuable in political discussion as it was difficult to contradict. Parliament did need to be managed.

It is not simply deceit in convoluted political manoeuvres that explains the central enigma of Hanoverian politics: the apparent need of ministers in secure control of Parliament, *and* confident that this control would not be challenged by the electoral process, to consider the attitudes and activities of the opposition, both within and without Parliament. This need appears to vindicate the recent stress on extra-parliamentary agitation, and can be seen at work in the chronology of political disturbances outlined earlier in the chapter. The process apparently culminated in the collapse of the Newcastle ministry in 1756. Unlike that of Walpole in 1742, it was not affected by electoral defeat, for the 1754 general election had been a triumph for the government. Nevertheless it apparently fell as a result of the popular agitation over the humiliating loss of Minorca to the French. The situation in 1756 was in fact more complex. Though Fox's inability to stand up to Pitt, whom he was frightened of, in debate was very important, the likely parliamentary storm over Minorca also brought to a head the question of relations between Newcastle and Henry Fox, the manager of the Commons, and thus created a crisis of parliamentary management irrespective of the activities of the opposition. Thus, the crisis of 1756 echoed those of 1742, 1744 and 1746: the government was divided. Under these circumstances, it was important for politicians to consider how best to create a new stable ministerial alignment, and in this context it was felt necessary to consider the views of parliamentarians and to take note of the public debate over policy. Many parliamentarians had opinions on policy; they were not simply manoeuvring to their own personal or factional advantage. As Parliament was the public forum in which the ministry formally presented and defended its policy and was criticised in a fashion that obliged it to reply, it was Parliament where the public debate over policy can be seen as most intense and effective. There was an obligation to respond that was lacking in the world of print, and an immediate linkage between the debates and the taking of decisions, the debates themselves being occasioned by the discussion of these very decisions. Thus the financial power of Parliament, the need to turn to it in order to obtain the finance necessary for policy, gave it a role in the field of policy, especially foreign policy, that it otherwise lacked.

The extent to which this role was exercised in an informed fashion, and to which Parliament had a competence in the field of particular aspects of policy and was therefore able to exercise a general supervisory role, is difficult to assess. A major problem is presented by the nature of the sources for parliamentary debates, which themselves throw light on the political culture of the period. The sources do not provide, and did not offer contemporaries, a complete account of the debates and the accuracy of what was provided is also questionable. This was due to the restrictive policies of Parliament itself (Doc. 29). In 1738 restrictions were toughened, in 1741 the publication of recent debates in book form led to the imprisonment of the printer and in 1747, as a result of action on behalf of those who held the privilege of printing the Jacobite treason trials conducted by the Lords, the *Gentleman's Magazine* stopped parliamentary reporting, while the attribution of speeches to individual Members in the *London Magazine* ceased. There was little sense among parliamentarians in the first half of the century that the people were entitled to a full, reliable and rapid account of debates.

The unreliable nature of the sources that do exist was a problem for contemporaries and historians, but, in part, reflects the extent of politicisation and the realisation that producing partisan accounts of debates might influence the national political audience (Doc. 30). Some division lists were published, and this was especially the case in election years. *A Guide to the Electors of Great Britain*, prepared for the 1722 election, recorded the votes of MPs on the crucial Peerage Bill of 1719, while the *List of those who were For and Against bringing in the Excise Bill* (1733) was produced in the hope of affecting the forthcoming general election. The mid-century fall in the political temperature led to a decrease in the number of division lists, both manuscript ones for parliamentary management and printed ones for electoral propaganda. Publication of reports of debates reflected public interest and, alongside criticisms, such magazine reports were certainly treated as accurate by some parliamentarians. John Campbell MP recorded of the Commons debate on 1 December 1742, 'Mr. Carew had got a magazine in which Mr. Sandys speech upon the motion for removing Sir Robert Walpole from His Majesty's person and councils was printed. He held it in his hand and read most of it very distinctly as part of his own speech.' Thus the hypocrisy of Sandys, once a bitter critic of Walpole, now a member of a government protecting him from parliamentary attack, could be clearly demonstrated. Later that month, John Tucker MP informed his brother that he had been greatly impressed by the debates on the Hanoverian subsidies, adding 'I shall not endeavour to particularise them because I expect one side at least of them if not both will be soon in print from whence you will see what has been said.'[22]

Parliamentary sources are worse for years of relative political quiescence, such as 1723–5 and 1747–53, and best for periods of volatility and marked tension. It was then that parliamentarians were both most likely to attend and most likely to report on proceedings, or at least to seek to supplement the printed sources. It was also then that these sources were likely to be most comprehensive as the pressure of public interest was strongest. The publication of parliamentary sources reflected particular peaks of crisis and attention.

One of the most valuable points to emerge from a consideration of parliamentary correspondence is the uncertainty of parliamentarians concerning likely developments. This uncertainty
was most marked in times of war, reflecting the general volatility
of these periods. In addition, this uncertainty indicates the danger of placing too much weight on the public, especially printed,
debate over policy. That suggested a false clarity over policy, in
which diplomatic and military strategies were predetermined by
partisan political traditions, the weight of history interacting
with specific and clashing partisan viewpoints. Thus, particular
views could be regarded as Tory, Whig, Country or Patriot and
they could be associated with distinct policies.

Such an analysis was and is misleading. It was employed to
serve partisan points, usually in terms of arguments about consistency or, more commonly, inconsistency. However, the
striking feature of much contemporary parliamentary correspondence is the extent to which it was by no means clear to parliamentarians what policy would be followed, or how policies were
related to political groups. This was most apparent at points of
discontinuity, which were both domestic (changes in monarch or
ministry) and international (the outbreak of war and the negotia-
tions for peace). These could combine to produce a serious discontinuity, such as occurred in 1741–2, with the outbreak of war
on the Continent and the fall of the Walpole ministry (Doc. 31).
This was not simply the hesitation of an MP faced by a change
of ministry, but rather the uncertainty provoked by a volatile
situation in which the views of most politicians were unclear and
their alignments changing. Indeed the very stress on consistency
that characterised much of the public debate reflected its general
absence, or rather the difficulty of defining and maintaining a
consistent position and persuading others that this had been
done in a rapidly changing world. It was possible for one group
to be, at least in part, reasonably consistent: in opposition from
1714 most of the Tories continued to denounce the political
system as corrupt and maintained a resolutely isolationist attitude. The Tories, however, had to face two differing problems.
Those who were Jacobite in inclination had to consider what
changes they wished to encourage in order to facilitate the success of their cause and had to consider the particular conception
of national interests that Jacobitism entailed. The Tories as a

whole had to determine how best to further their aims of opposition to the ministry. Effective opposition required co-operation with dissident Whigs. This was the lesson of the period 1714–42, and in the early 1740s the Tories sought to further their ends by such methods. This helped to account for the ferocity of the attacks on Hanoverian subsidies in 1742–4 and on the Hanoverian commitment more generally in the early 1740s. Hanover seemed an issue on which Tories and opposition Whigs could unite. In October 1743 the influential Tory Bishop of Salisbury wrote to an Under-Secretary, 'you see already that the distinction for this winter is to be *Hanoverians* and *Englishmen*. If occasion has been given for this distinction, the Hanoverians will be hard set in an English Parliament'.[23]

However, even over the Hanover issue there were serious differences, for again a powerful lesson of the period 1714–42 was that of the transience of 'Country' co-operation. The ideology and polemic of co-operation between Tories and opposition Whigs joined in a 'Country' opposition to a corrupt ministry, whose self-servedness encompassed an abject failure to defend national interests in the face of Hanoverian wishes, did not describe the reality of clashing traditions and views and the stubborn maintenance of differing Tory and opposition Whig legacies. This was especially apparent, the opposition Whigs failing to share Tory hostility to Dissent, over ecclesiastical issues in 1718–19 and 1736, but it was also obvious in differing responses to British neutrality in the War of the Polish Succession in 1733–5. The Hanover issue of 1742–4 in large part obscured differences between the Tories and the opposition Whigs, but it also raised one important distinction, that between those who supported the Protestant Succession, which now meant the Hanoverian dynasty, and the Jacobites who opposed it. To that extent, the parliamentary discussion of Hanoverian issues was not totally unsatisfactory for the ministry. These issues led to differences between Tories and opposition Whigs. In December 1741, the Jacobite MP Lord Charles Noel Somerset, 'moved that a clause should be added to it desiring His Majesty not to engage this Kingdom in a war for any dominions not belonging to the Crown of Great Britain, but this amendment was disapproved by Mr. Pulteney himself and withdrawn by the proposer'.[24] William Pulteney, the opposition Whig leader, who essentially sought a reconstitution of the ministry, was more concerned about royal views and the likely exigencies of office, which certainly would include sensitivity to Hanoverian interests. The betrayal of the 'Country' platform in 1742 as many of the opposition Whigs joined in a reconstitution of a Whig-only ministry, without insisting on the political reforms they had called for while in opposition to Walpole, was to lead to Tory disenchantment and a partial withdrawal from discussion of politics by Tory parliamentarians, so that some debates were largely occasions for an exchange of views between Whigs. Ministries remained Whig, the Tories continued in opposition.

Issues were definitely important in the 1740s, issues of competence and of policy, and they played a major role in the manoeuvres of politicians for office. The combination of a revived Jacobite threat and of French success in the War of the Austrian Succession constituted what was truly a mid-eighteenth-century crisis, and helped to produce a considerable measure of Whig unity, the consolidation in 1744–6 of the Pelham ministry, based on widespread Whig support. The creation of this ministry, the defeat of the Jacobites, the government's sweeping success in the 1747 general election, and the negotiation of acceptable peace terms in 1748 after arguably the most unsuccessful war since Charles I's with France in 1626–9, all helped to lower the political temperature. Parliamentary attendance slackened (Doc. 32) as the political situation eased. There was a strong sense that existing policies and personnel would last until the ministerial revolution that was expected to follow the eventual accession of the Prince of Wales as King Frederick I.[25] The attention of foreign diplomats, an important gauge of the perception of the location of political power, was concentrated on Court and ministry, not Parliament.

The anticipated domestic discontinuity did not occur, for, far from the elderly George II dying, his elder son, Frederick, predeceased him in 1751. Indeed George II, born in 1683, was to live longer than any previous monarch, which, given the political role of the monarch, was of fundamental political importance. Instead, it was the death of Pelham (1754) and the coming of war with France, the early stages of which were not successful, that produced a major discontinuity. The parliamentary consequences of the parlous international position in 1755–6 should

88

not, however, be over-emphasised. It was the crisis *within* the government that was so serious in 1755–7. Parliamentary debates were of consequence in so far as they influenced this crisis, providing opportunities for trials of strength. Once that crisis had been resolved in the shape of the stable Newcastle–Pitt ministry, then Parliament became of less political consequence, though it remained significant as an important component of the system of assured public finance that enabled the British government to fight the Seven Years' War with such persistence. Parliament might have been the scene for more serious attacks on the ministry, had the limited military success of 1755–7 not been transformed into glorious victory, but, as a consequence of both victory and ministerial stability, Parliament was quiescent, certainly compared to the situation during the Nine Years' War and the War of the Spanish Succession. Governmental unity was lost in 1761–2, with the crises that led to the resignations of first Pitt and then Newcastle, but their hesitation in attacking the new ministry, the general desire for peace, the initial popularity of the new king (George II had died in 1760) and the government's success in both war and peace blunted the force of parliamentary and political criticism. The Peace of Paris (1763) encountered more parliamentary attacks than that of Aix-la-Chapelle (1748) had done, a measure of the stronger sense that Britain had had a bad deal, but the situation was essentially the same (Doc. 33). The ministry carried the Address of Thanks on 9 December 1762 by 319 to 65, and there was no division in the Lords. As so often in Hanoverian Britain, it was the parliamentary strength of the government, rather than the vigour of its critics, that was most strikingly apparent to observers, both domestic and foreign, and their view of ministerial power owed much to this strength.

Bute, however, proved a broken reed. Although the ministry enjoyed solid majorities in both Houses of Parliament, Bute, whose enthusiasm for high office had always been tempered, found the stress of politics unbearable.[26] He was replaced as First Lord of the Treasury by George Grenville, whom George III soon found arrogant and overbearing.[27] George himself was acutely irritable, possibly as a result of poor health. In 1765 the king was able to dispense with Grenville, though his replacement, Charles Watson-Wentworth, the 2nd Marquess of Rockingham, was not

89

much to his wishes. The new ministry sought to defuse the political problems created by earlier attempts to tackle the government's financial problems. The strains of paying for the Seven Years' War, never appreciated sufficiently by the bellicose Pitt and his supporters, had forced the ministers of the early 1760s to think of retrenchment and new taxation. Both had led to political difficulties, the first in the debate surrounding the ending of the conflict, the second initially with the unpopular cider tax of 1763 and then with the Stamp Act of 1765. The crisis over the Grenville ministry's Stamp Act, which imposed a series of duties in the North American colonies, was greater than that over the cider tax, repealed in 1766, because it raised the question of parliamentary authority in America. Concerned about the violent response in America and influenced by pressure from British merchants, worried about an American commercial blockade, the Rockinghamites repealed the Stamp Act, despite the reluctance of George III.[28]

The Rockingham ministry suffered not only from royal disfavour but also from division, and in July 1766 George III, hoping 'to extricate this country out of faction', sent for Pitt. The Pitt ministry was not, however, a success, in part because Pitt's acceptance of a peerage as Earl of Chatham weakened his control of the Commons. The dearth of Commons leadership was an important aspect of 1760s instability, which was related closely to the ending of Old Corps Whig cohesion. It is difficult to imagine Walpole, or even Pelham, losing control as their successors in the 1760s were to do.[29] The sickly Pitt became an invalid in the spring of 1767, in part probably as a consequence of stress and depression, but the ministry of the Duke of Grafton which followed that of Pitt was also weak and divided. Nevertheless, once George III had found an effective parliamentary manager in Lord North,[30] the political situation, and Parliament's role within it, were then quiescent until the unprecedented crisis produced by Cornwallis's surrender at Yorktown (1781), the defeat of the attempt to reconquer America. George III was forced to turn to a political grouping that he distrusted, the Rockinghamites, who were pledged to independence for America. The 'civil revolutions',[31] changes in government in 1782–3, helped to contribute to a sense of political failure, even collapse (Doc. 34), that suggests that contemporary expectations of the political system were not of frequent changes of government in response to shifts in parliamentary and electoral opinion, but rather of a stable ministry responsive to, and thus, if necessary, limited by, responsible parliamentary and popular opinion. This assumption was shared abroad, where rulers such as Catherine II (the Great) of Russia, Frederick II (the Great) of Prussia and Joseph II of Austria, argued in the early 1780s that Britain was weak, that this was due to inherent characteristics of her political system which would probably lead to the dissolution of her empire, and that her weakness made her an undesirable ally.

The resolution of the crisis in the shape of the stable Pitt ministry was far from inevitable. It was not certain that Pitt would secure a Commons majority because George III had appointed him to office in December 1783, and George's action brought out the lack of agreement about the constitution, the fluidity of constitutional conventions, that tends all too often to be forgotten. George's actions, which were regarded by some as unconstitutional, were countered by a collective resignation of office holders, similar to the step that had forced George II to abandon his attempt to create a ministry under Earl Granville (Carteret) in February 1746, or the resignation of Rockingham's supporters in protest at the appointment of William, 2nd Earl of Shelburne in July 1782. Commons defeats in January 1784 led Pitt to think of resigning and George III to reiterate his willingness to abdicate.[32] An attempt by independent MPs to create a broad-based government of national union, a frequently-expressed aspiration during the century that reflected widespread suspicion of what was seen as the factious nature of party politics, gave Pitt breathing space. His position was improved further by a swelling tide of favourable public opinion, betokened by a large number of addresses from counties and boroughs, with over 50,000 signatures in total, in favour of George III and the free exercise of the royal prerogative in choosing ministers.[33] Thus, the formation of the Pitt government had not ended the crisis created by the poor relations between George III and the Fox–North ministry that had replaced that of Shelburne, but it had changed its nature, made it more public and brought monarch and government on to the same side. The more public nature of the transformed crisis led to an upsurge in popular interest and this focused on support for George, itself a testimony to the potential popularity of the monarchy, and thus for his new ministers. Parliament was dissolved when Pitt felt able to face a general election, and the elections, many of which were contested on national political grounds,[34] were very favourable for the ministry.

The crisis of 1783–4 thus demonstrated that, alongside Parliament's undoubted importance, it was also necessary to consider that of the Crown and of circumstances that could affect both, not least by giving weight to extra-parliamentary influences. Ministries that won general elections could fall soon after: Newcastle's overwhelming success in the election of 1754, and North's in that of 1780, did not prevent their fall from office in 1756 and 1782. Victory in a general election differed from the modern situation. Many seats were not contested on national political grounds, while the nature of political parties was also different: in the eighteenth century they tended to lack an identifiable national leadership, an organised constituent membership and a recognised corpus of policy and principle around which to cohere and which could serve to link local activists to national activity. Before concluding that the term party should not be applied, it is necessary to note that many modern parties, as in France, India, Italy and the United States, are monolithic neither in organisation nor in policy.

Historians have disagreed substantially over the nature of party in the eighteenth century. Older views of a world of natural parties were challenged in 1929 with the publication of Lewis Namier's *The Structure of Politics at the Accession of George III*. In place of party and ideology, Namier emphasised patronage, corruption and (self-)interest. He discussed the extent of political influence, the number of placemen and the secret service accounts through which support was apparently purchased by the government. Namier's work was very influential in studies of the period back to the 1740s and up to the 1780s, but from the 1960s on it became more common to stress ideology and issues as causes of political configurations. This led to a re-evaluation of the role of party, and the concept now plays a major role, especially in writing on the reigns of Anne, George I and George II. It is now easier to appreciate eighteenth-century parties on their own terms, rather than as unsatisfactory anticipations of modern equivalents. Part of the problem is that it is inappropriate to offer an analysis that is equally pertinent throughout the century. Furthermore, parties played very different roles, firstly in the formation of ministries, secondly in the maintenance or weakening of parliamentary majorities, and thirdly in elections and in the country at large. They were generally more important in political battles in the Commons than in the world of Court and Cabinet; while in the country at large the intensity of the party struggle, and, to a certain extent, political alignments, varied considerably.

Though firm control over a disciplined parliamentary party was absent, ministries that had won an election were likely to be longer-lasting than those that had not had an opportunity to do so. An absence or loss of royal favour could, however, be fatal, as Godolphin discovered in 1710, Newcastle in 1762, Grenville in 1765, Rockingham in 1766, Fox–North in 1783 and Pitt in 1801. In 1783–4 George III rejected the requests for peerage creations made by the Fox–North ministry and then changed tack in order to help Pitt, an obvious demonstration of the direction and importance of royal favour.[35] Failure in war could also play a major role in the fall of ministries, as with those of Newcastle (1756) and North.

Backed by the king and both houses of Parliament, and with clear popular support, Pitt the Younger's government might therefore appear secure, but parliamentary checks throw light on the nature of eighteenth-century politics, and specifically the party system. In 1785 the ministry was defeated over the Westminster scrutiny, a division that ensured that Charles James Fox, the leading opposition MP, was returned for such a prominent seat. That year the ministry withdrew its proposals for a new commercial and financial relationship between England and Ireland in the face of serious opposition from the Irish House of Commons. The proposals had earlier been substantially modified in the face of British mercantile and parliamentary hostility. In 1786 the British House of Commons rejected a plan for fortifying the country's leading naval dockyards.

Defeats occurred not because of the strength of the opposition, but because on specific issues the ministry lost the support of the influential and numerous independent MPs (Doc. 35). Whereas in the first half of the century there had been a fundamentally two-party Whig–Tory alignment, albeit one in which the role of opposition Whigs was often crucial, from the 1760s, and particularly in that decade, the situation was more loose and shifting. Commons support for the government rested not on a party but on a coalition of first, the 'party of the crown, comprising members of the Commons whose primary interest lay in public or court service, and whose overriding loyalties were to the sovereign and to the principle that the King's government must be carried on'; secondly, groups of active politicians seeking power each with their own followers; and thirdly, independent MPs, essentially concerned with local interests but willing to offer loyal, though not uncritical, support. Opposition comprised critical independents and groups of excluded politicians.[36] The role of competing personal groups, operating without the semi-imperatives of fear and loyalty created by the Jacobite challenge and the response to it, helped to produce ministerial and parliamentary insecurity in the 1760s, while, throughout the reign of George III, it was necessary to consider the role of the independent MPs. Their existence and role reflected the limited nature of the party configuration in Parliament. Independents rarely took the initiative in matters of national politics, and generally gave their support to the Crown and the ministers who enjoyed the confidence of the monarch, which was why George III's withdrawal of his backing from the Fox–North government in 1783 had been so crucial in the Lords. They were, however, willing to withdraw support over particular issues, and this represented an important, but unpredictable, constraint on government policy. Lord Walsingham expressed his concern to Pitt in July 1786 about 'a loose House of Commons, whose firm and systematic support is not to be depended upon in the way which it must be had to carry on a war effectually'.[37] In some crises, such as that posed by the apparent rise of French-inspired domestic radicalism in 1792, the independents would back the Crown, but in 1782 they had withdrawn their support from North, in early 1784 many preferred to pursue the chimera of a broad-based, apparently national government, and in 1791 they forced Pitt to back down when war with Russia seemed imminent.

In the Lords, the 'Party of the Crown', composed of archbishops, bishops, royal household officers, Scottish representative peers and newly created or promoted peers, provided a consistent basis for the ministerial majority.[38] Thus, a chamber that had posed considerable problems of management during the reign of Anne became the most quiescent of the two houses of Parliament: patronage was applied in a consistent fashion to unite the 'Party of the Crown', while co-operation between Crown and ministry and an absence of issues as controversial as those of the succession, the Church and foreign policy during the reign of Anne kept tension to a minimum, though there could be crises as in late 1783.

If the Crown and the independents were, in their different ways, both important potential constraints on the government's room for political manoeuvre, this was also true of divisions within the ministry. These had been important in the shifting politics of the 1760s, but their decline in significance was both cause and consequence of the more stable North and Pitt governments. In this context, clear royal support for the leading minister was especially important. In 1784–92 the Pitt government was divided over a number of issues, most obviously proposals for parliamentary reform and the abolition of the slave trade, the fortification bill and the parliamentary trial of Warren Hastings. Unlike, however, earlier in the century, such ministerial divisions did not become prominent in Parliament. This suggests that possibly in light of George III's attitude, ministers were prepared to restrict their differences, and that, as the political system under the Pitt ministry was less fluid than it had been in, for example, 1714–21, 1739–51, 1762–9 and 1782–4, this encouraged ministerial cohesion.

By 1792 the ministers were to be facing a new challenge, the apparently combined forces of domestic radicalism and the French Revolution. In considering how they faced these potent threats it is necessary first to assess the background of eighteenth-century extra-parliamentary activity.

Notes

1   Thomas, *The House of Commons in the Eighteenth Century* (Oxford, 1971); C. Jones ed., *Party and Management in Parliament, 1660–1784* (Leicester, 1984).

2   Though see M. W. McCahill, *Order and Equipoise: the Peerage and the House of Lords 1783–1806* (1978); C. and D. L. Jones eds., *Peers,*

Politics and Power: the House of Lords, 1603–1911 (1986), and C. Jones ed., *A Pillar of the Constitution: the House of Lords in British politics, 1640–1784* (1989).

3   Rogers, *Whigs and Cities*, p. 397.

4   Woodfine, 'The Anglo-Spanish War of 1739', in Black ed., *The Origins of War in Early Modern Europe* (Edinburgh, 1987), pp. 185–92.

5   Brewer, *Party Ideology*.

6   Perry, *Public Opinion, Propaganda, and Politics*.

7   P. Woodland, 'Extra-parliamentary political organization in the making: Benjamin Heath and the opposition to the 1763 Cider Excise', and 'Political atomization and regional interests in the 1761 Parliament: The impact of the cider debates, 1763–1766', *Parliamentary History* IV (1985) and VIII (1989).

8   K. Wilson, 'Empire, trade and popular politics in mid-Hanoverian Britain: the case of Admiral Vernon', *Past and Present*, CXXI (November 1988), p. 77.

9   Thorne ed., *The House of Commons* i, 335; McCahill, *Order and Equipoise*, pp. 90–112; Handley, 'Local legislative initiatives'; Innes, 'Parliament and the shaping of eighteenth-century English social policy', *Transactions of the Royal Historical Society*, 5th ser., XL (1990), pp. 63–92.

10   L. Davison, T. Hitchcock, T. Keirn and Shoemaker eds., *Stilling the Grumbling Hive: the response to social and economic problems in England, 1689–1750* (Stroud, 1992).

11   On foreign policy and politics, Black, *A System of Ambition? British foreign policy 1660–1793* (Harlow, 1991).

12   HMC., *Diary of the First Earl of Egmont* (3 vols., 1920–3) ii, 150; *St James's Chronicle*, 18 April 1769; Duke to Duchess of Newcastle, 10 December 1741, BL. Add. 33073 fo. 186.

13   Holmes, *British Politics in the Age of Anne* (1967).

14   D. Szechi, *Jacobitism and Tory Politics* (Edinburgh, 1984); B. Hill, *Robert Harley* (New Haven, 1988).

15   W. A. Speck, 'The Whig schism under George I', *Huntington Library Quarterly*, XL (1977), pp. 171–9; R. Hatton, *George I: Elector and King* (1978), pp. 192–202; Black, 'Parliament and the political and diplomatic crisis of 1717–18', *Parliamentary History*, III (1984), pp. 77–101.

16   Hutcheson to Earl Cowper, 20 April 1722, Hertford CRO. D/EP F55 fo. 51; Anon., *Gulliver Decypher'd* (1727), p. 38.

17   Caesar Diary, BL. Add. 62558 fo. 49.

18   J. B. Owen, *The Rise of the Pelhams* (1957).

19   Warwick, CRO. CR136 B 2530/22.

20   Luff, 'Henry Fox and the "lead" in the House of Commons

1754–1755', *Parliamentary History*, VI (1987), pp. 33–46.

21 E. J. S. Fraser, 'The Pitt–Newcastle coalition and the conduct of the Seven Years War 1757–1760' (D. Phil., Oxford, 1976); Peters, *Pitt and Popularity: the patriot minister and London opinion during the Seven Years War* (Oxford, 1980).

22 D. Hayton and C. Jones eds., *A Register of Parliamentary Lists 1660–1761* (Leicester, 1979) and . . . *Supplement* (Leicester, 1982); John to Pryse Campbell, 2 December 1742, Carmarthen, Dyfed Record Office, Cawdor Muniments, Box 138; John to Richard Tucker, 14 December 1742, Bod. MS. Don. c. 105 fo. 197; M. Ransome, 'The reliability of contemporary reporting of the debates of the House of Commons', *Bulletin of the Institute of Historical Research*, XIX (1942–3), pp. 67–79; Black, 'A Diplomat visits Parliament: an unprinted account of the army estimates debate of 1733', *Parliamentary History*, V (1986), pp. 101–5, and 'Parliamentary reporting in England in the early eighteenth century', *Parliaments, Estates and Representation*, VII (1987), pp. 61–9.

23 Thomas Sherlock to Edward Weston, 8 October 1743, Farmington, Lewis Walpole Library, Weston papers vol. 3.

24 Philip Yorke MP to Marchioness Grey, 8 December 1741, Bedford CRO. L30/9/113/4. 'It' was the Address.

25 The Prince's policies can be followed in Newman, 'Leicester House politics, 1749–51', *English Historical Review*, LXXVI (1961), pp. 577–89, and 'Leicester House politics, 1750–60, from the papers of John, Second Earl of Egmont', Royal Historical Society, *Camden Miscellany* Camden 4th ser. VII (1969), pp. 85–213.

26 Schweizer ed., *Lord Bute: essays in re-interpretation* (Leicester, 1988).

27 P. Lawson, *George Grenville* (Oxford, 1984).

28 Langford, *The First Rockingham Administration, 1765–1766* (Oxford, 1973), pp. 109–98; Thomas, *British Politics and the Stamp Act Crisis: the first phase of the American Revolution, 1763–1767* (Oxford, 1975).

29 Brooke, *The Chatham Administration* (1956).

30 Thomas, *Lord North* (1976).

31 Lord Grantham, Foreign Secretary, to Sir Robert Murray Keith, envoy in Vienna, 22 February 1783, BL. Add. 35528 fo. 22.

32 George III to Pitt, 13 January 1784, PRO. 30/8/103 fo. 30.

33 Cannon, *The Fox–North Coalition: crisis of the constitution* (Cambridge, 1969), pp. 178–96.

34 O'Gorman, *Voters, Patrons and Parties*, pp. 295–6.

35 W. C. Lowe, 'George III, peerage creations and politics, 1760–1784', *Historical Journal*, XXXV (1992), pp. 606–8.

36 I. R. Christie, 'Party in politics in the age of Lord North's administration', *Parliamentary History*, VI (1987), pp. 47–8, 62.

37   Walsingham to Pitt, 16 July 1786, Cambridge, University Library, Add. 6958.

38   D. Large, 'The decline of the "Party of the Crown" and the rise of parties in the House of Lords, 1783–1837', *English Historical Review*, LXXVIII (1963), pp. 669–95.

5

Politics out of doors

The notion of development that is central to much historical analysis is itself judgemental (or not value-free to use another ugly modern term). A combination of the Whig myth of history and the concept of political Darwinism (that the best-suited to its environment wins out), ensured that the development of the modern political system, first parliamentary government and then democratisation, seemed the major theme in British history and was thus automatically associated with progress. The eighteenth century could be readily understood in such a schema. It was the period between the establishment of parliamentary government thanks to the Glorious Revolution and the nineteenth-century moves towards (male) democratisation, beginning with the First Reform Act in 1832. This analysis was linked with a shift in sympathies: the aristocrats who acquired praise by defying James II were replaced by descendants who could be stigmatised for benefiting from stagnation, if not corruption, and for resisting reform. The place of opinion 'out of doors', outside the world of Court and Parliament, was similarly clear. Its development indicated the limits of the representative system, and, in turn, helped eventually to secure its failure.

Such an analysis was, in part, an aspect of the important role of history as public myth, but, as already suggested, it has grave limitations. These are both methodological and empirical (factual). The notion of development in a given direction is suspect anyway, but even more so is the attempt to treat a struggle for change in the political system as the central political issue. Rather than focusing on attempts to change the distribution of power within society as significant, as they indeed were under the stress of a revolutionary situation in the 1790s and thereafter, it is more appropriate to understand the extent to which those active in politics, both in and outside the élite, earlier chose generally to work within the system. This can be better appreciated if the absence of a revolutionary consciousness is not treated as a sign of failure. Indeed, in the period 1685–1746 'radicalism' could be found almost exclusively not with proto-democrats but with those who sought to change the monarch: Monmouth in 1685, William III in 1688–9, the Jacobites thereafter.

The social changes of the period can scarcely provide an alternative route to 'modern' radicalism. Though London, the most populous city in western Europe, had a sophisticated citizenry, supporting for example the largest newspaper press in Europe prior to revolutionary Paris, and though the pace of economic change was obvious from mid-century, there was scant sign of the emergence of any fully-articulated and comprehensive class system. Instead, the urban population shared in the spectrum of existing opinion and was divided by confessional, economic and political views. This lack of urban homogeneity aided integration with the rest of society and ensured that urban interests could be wooed by élite politicians (Doc. 36). The urban dimension of politics can be emphasised, not least because of the location of so many parliamentary seats in towns (albeit, often small places), and the very specific and important economic interests towns had, which could be furthered by political means. A town's use of its MPs to advance or defend their local interests with government or in Parliament, especially in relation to the passage of Acts of Parliament, provided the basis for a strong relationship, that required both parties to give and take. Thus, at that level, politics was reactive and consensual, searching for compromise as part of a dynamic relationship in which local issues were crucial. This relationship between MPs and towns, and the recognition on the part of both sides that the relationship had to be constantly nurtured, was a long-term structural feature of politics that added stability to the system.

There were, however, particular problems in managing large urban constituencies. 'Radicalism' as generally understood was particularly associated with large towns, especially London. It would, however, be misleading to see such radicalism as continuously increasing. Indeed, once the Wilkite controversy and the American War were over, there was a great dip in the activities and popularity of radicalism.

It would, however, be mistaken to think of extra-parliamentary politics primarily in terms of popular mass action and radicalism. Aside from noting the analytical problem of determining what is radical and what conservative – how, for example, the Jewish Naturalisation Act agitation or that over the Cider Excise are to be conceptualised – it is also clear both that much popular action can be defined as 'conservative', and that extra-parliamentary action was not simply a matter of popular mass action. The conservatism can be found in explicitly political action, most obviously the anti-revolutionary loyalism of the 1790s; and also in what has been presented as the 'moral economy' of the populace, their support for customary rights and charges.[1] Support for government policies could be just as significant and valid an expression of public opinion as opposition to them, and this became more clearly the case in the last quarter of the century, first with backing for a firm line towards the American colonists. Far from popular conservatism of an explicitly political character diminishing with time, it was to be a major feature from the 1790s on, the Loyalist Association followed by a plethora of organisations that can be described as populist right-wing: Constitutional Associations, Protestant Associations, Pitt Clubs, Loyalist Associations, True Blue Clubs, Wellington Clubs, Brunswick Clubs, British Orange Societies. These served as the counterpart to the radical societies of the 1790s and early nineteenth century, and are a reminder of the need to stress the diversity and complexity of public opinion.

Extra-parliamentary political action was both an aspect of the traditional multi-faceted political world, one in which institutions such as town councils could play a role, and a reflection of new or developing features. The latter included most obviously the greatly expanded role of the press, as well as the rising importance of national lobby and interest groups.[2] More generally, these reflected, though they were not limited by, urbanisation, professionalisation and the broadening strata of the middling orders in society. Care was taken to keep these groups informed of political developments and to win their support.

Petitions, meetings and print were all aspects of an interactive political world, one in which widespread interest and commitment were necessary and present. Thus a general meeting of the Yorkshire freeholders on 25 March 1784 heard speeches from candidates in the general election, including William Wilberforce, and accepted an address condemning Fox's East India bill and justifying the dismissal of the Fox–North ministry as a 'just exertion' of the royal prerogative. The proceedings then appeared as a pamphlet published in York. The impact of certain politicians on opinion outside the heart of politics played a major role not only in eliciting and channelling popular political views, but also, though more episodically, on the course of high politics. Thus, Pitt the Elder owed his importance in the political manoeuvres of 1765–6 in large part to the sense that he was crucial to governmental stability and popularity, though in practice he was in many respects inadequate to the new demands, in both politics and policy, of the 1760s.

Two features of the world 'out of doors' can be focused on: first, the continued role of confessional (religious) identity and issues and secondly the growth, with the press, of the means for mass, anonymous political expression. Secularisation should not be emphasised. The division between Anglicanism and Dissent that had played such a major role in the dynamic of Whig–Tory struggle, especially in 1689–1720 (though it must be stressed that many Whigs were Anglicans), was still important thereafter. Dissenters played a major role in pro-American agitation in the 1770s and were initially more sympathetic to the French Revolution than other groups. As the Test and Corporation Acts survived the 1689–1720 period of controversy and change, so Anglican prerogatives and privileges became a permanent feature of the Whig state; unlike in the mid seventeenth century, it was possible to remove the Stuarts without overthrowing Anglicanism. It also proved possible to install a Lutheran monarch (George I) without apparent damage to the Church of England. As a consequence of the Church's maintenance of its position, pressure for the repeal of the Acts, the political face of Dissent, itself came to denote opposition to the dominant system. This was especially serious given the stress on religion that characterised much of the ideological response to the de-christianizing French Revolutionaries (Doc. 37). Indeed the revival of Toryism as a coherent political position in the late eighteenth century has been associated with the defence of the Church.[3] A religious foundation to English electoral behaviour in the later eighteenth century has also recently been emphasised and the rift between Anglican and Dissenter has been regarded as essential both to the continued nature of local political divisions and, towards the end of the century, to the configuration of the national division between the ministry of William Pitt the Younger and the Whig opposition.[4] Religion has also been seen as playing a central part in political motivation in Ireland and Scotland.[5]

Diversity was, however, the keynote. Thus, a recent study of the Vale of Nailsworth, an area of rural industry and evangelical Nonconformity, has emphasised how in the late eighteenth and early nineteenth centuries there was an 'essential compatibility between Nonconformity and the Establishment . . . a spirit of cooperation, fostered by Chapel leaders and supported . . . by lay Anglican lords, rested on a Whiggish belief in tolerance and a social foundation of class collaboration'. Whig Anglicans were mostly Low Church, and the bulk of the Presbyterians who were absorbed into the Church of England after 1689 swelled the numbers of the Low Church. Similarly, work on Protestant–Catholic relations has emphasised acceptance as well as tension.[6]

The growth of the press was striking.[7] The eighteenth century witnessed a massive expansion in total sales and the number of titles, as well as the first daily, Sunday and provincial papers. The appearance of London dailies marked the creation of a regular and responsive world of printed news, interacting with political events far more closely than was possible with pamphlets, books or even weekly newspapers. From the early 1770s, parliamentary reporting came to play an accepted and regular role in the press, as the attempt to prevent it collapsed in the face of serious controversy.[8] During the session, such reporting took up much of the non-advertising space in the press. The Dublin Parliament also attracted attention, and not just in the columns of the press. Thus, the debate of 12 August 1785 on Anglo-Irish trade was reported in a 200-page book published in Dublin.

The early provincial press was very important in distributing metropolitan news and news of foreign affairs. Most local newspapers consisted largely of material pirated from the London press. Thus this 'provincial press' in its first flush was actually spreading metropolitan opinion rather than reflecting local views. This played a major role in the development of national political campaigns, such as the Wilkite movement, the county petitioning movements of the early 1780s for economical and parliamentary reform, anti-slavery, the organisation of Lord George Gordon's Protestant Association and the campaigns of 1787–90 against the Test and Corporation Acts. Provincial papers became more active in their expression of distinctive opinions, and many of them more obviously partisan in their politics. Newspaper reporting came to be seen as important in contested elections. Thus in 1768 the leading Edinburgh paper, the *Caledonian Mercury*, carried a report about the Cromartyshire election that criticised the process by which William Pulteney had beaten Sir John Gordon. Pulteney felt obliged to reply, and the next issue carried his letter accordingly. It is significant that politicians competing for the support of a tiny electorate of fewer than twenty should have felt it important to create a favourable impression in the world of print (Doc. 38).

The press was central to the process of politicisation, the strengthening, sustaining and widening, if not of a specific political consciousness, then at least of national political awareness. In 1775 12.6 million newspaper stamps (showing that duty had been paid) were issued, a figure that was to rise to 16 million in 1801. The second half of the eighteenth century, however, was a period of development within an already existing model. If new titles were founded, headlining improved, the number of columns per page increased or the first Sunday papers launched, that essentially did not alter the nature of the press.

Indeed the late eighteenth century was essentially a period of limited change between two epochs of more fundamental importance. From 1695 to the mid-1740s, was a period of major change. Politically, the crucial fact was that the Licensing Act (requiring approval for publication), once it had lapsed in 1695, was not reintroduced. This created a context in which, rather than seeking to suppress opinion, political groups sought to foster favourable reporting. This was within certain parameters that excluded Jacobitism,[9] just as book publishing excluded blasphemy. Nevertheless, the marked level of criticism that was voiced, and that became more pronounced during the century,[10] was such that opposition to government policy could be freely encouraged, a position that differed from most Continental states. The political controversies of 1695–1701 were conducted in pamphlets rather than newspapers. It was not until the last years of Anne's reign that newspapers reflected political controversies to the extent that they had done during the Exclusion Crisis.

Economically, the early eighteenth century was a period of rising sales and increasing advertisements that encouraged the launching of new titles and new types, including daily and provincial newspapers. The period also saw the creation and ending of the illegal cheap and unstamped press.[11] The mid nineteenth century was to witness technological changes in news transmission and newspaper production and distribution, and the creation of a greater market with the ending of the 'taxes on knowledge', the restrictive newspaper fiscal regime of the British *ancien régime*. The consequence was extraordinary growth in sales and the resulting development of the press. Penny dailies were launched, the *Daily News* selling 150,000 copies daily by 1871, the *Daily Telegraph* 300,000 by 1888.

In comparison, an eighteenth-century London newspaper was considered a great success if it sold 10,000 copies a week (most influential papers then were weeklies), and 2,000 was a reasonable sale. The world of 'mass' or 'popular' politics made possible by the eighteenth-century press was, therefore, very different to the situation in the age of Disraeli and Gladstone, and it is possibly most appropriate to use the term 'public' politics, as that does not imply the massive numbers and politicisation of the bulk of the population suggested by the terms mass and popular. A smaller scale of activity is not, however, the same as a lack of consequence, and the role of the press, as part of the world of print, in fostering and sustaining a political world very different to that of the calculations of borough patronage, can be seen in the response to the French Revolution. The press played a major role in the rise in petitioning. In part as a result of the rise of extra-parliamentary associations, the presentation of petitions on national issues to Parliament rose considerably in the last quarter of the century. In the boroughs the number of signatories was about double that of electors, a clear indication of the extent to which the 'political nation' was not limited to the electorate. Instead, politics encompassed a considerable amount of activity by the more humble members of the community (though mostly men), and thus, to an extent, directed, expressed and contained their views.

Though the rising importance of the press deserves emphasis it would be misleading to suggest that it was a precondition for public awareness of parliamentary or other politics. In addition, the notion of representation by, and responsiveness of MPs to constituents was not dependent on this agency of public politics, though the growth of the press fostered it. In 1721 the Bishop of Lincoln referred to 'the fear the Members have to oppose the popular clamour, at a time when public elections are so near'.[12] A recent account has referred to 'the common touch which was essential to success in an open constituency even in the days of the unreformed electoral system, and which was possessed by all the major political magnates of pre-Union Ireland even though the essence of their strength had derived from close boroughs'. A magnate who lacked such a touch, for example, John, Marquess of Abercorn, suffered as an electioneer in the county seats. In Buckinghamshire, 'county politics rested on more than the decisions of cosy little caucases of county gentlemen'.[13] The total English electorate in 1790 was about 300,000, a sizeable number, the Irish county electorate in 1784 about 46,000 and the total Welsh electorate in 1790 less than 19,000. Some seats, however, were rarely contested. In 1790 only eight of the forty English counties were contested; in 1796 only four. There was no contest in Nottinghamshire between 1722 and 1832, in Shropshire between 1722 and 1831, in Dorset between 1727 and 1806, in Cheshire between 1734 and 1832, in Lancashire between 1747 and 1820 and in Staffordshire between 1747 and 1832. In 1790 only 66 of the 203 English boroughs were contested; in 1796 only 55.[14]

Nevertheless, it is possible in many constituencies to discern a return in the second half of the century to levels of politicisation after a measure of mid-eighteenth-century hiatus. After a fall in the number of contested elections, to reach a low point in England of 46 in 1761, the number rose again, the average for the three elections of 1768–80 being 75. 7, in contrast to figures of 110 for 1722–34 and 55.4 for 1741–54.[15] In England as a whole politicisation in the 1760s owed much to the Wilkite controversy, which was especially important for the London region. In Surrey, politicisation was associated with the rise of Joseph Mawbey, a Vauxhall vinegar distiller, who became MP for Southwark, a baronet, and eventually, despite opposition to him as a parvenu, MP for Surrey (1775–90). Mawbey, who on occasion supported Wilkes, benefited in elections from the willingness of freeholders to ignore the county's 'natural' leaders. The influence of the latter was further affected by changes in property distribution, which helped bring new gentry into the ranks of Surrey's MPs.[16] There were calls in Britain for substantial changes in the political system in the 1770s and early 1780s,[17] just as there had been during the reigns of George I and George II.[18] The Society of the Supporters of the Bill of Rights, established in 1769 by a group of London radicals, including John Horne Tooke and John Sawbridge, supported not only Wilkes but also political reform, specifically shorter parliaments and a redistribution of seats. This programme was continued by the Constitutional Society established in London in 1771. Fresh impetus to reform led in 1779–80 to the establishment of the Yorkshire Association and the Society for Constitutional Information. The former served in 1780 as a model for the establishment of reforming associations elsewhere, and Christopher Wyvill, a Yorkshire landowner, sought to create a co-ordinated movement. This led in 1780–1 to nationwide petitioning (60,000 signatures in 1780) and national conventions, but the divided movement achieved little. The Society, established in London in April 1780 by a group of Rational Dissenters, including John Cartwright and Thomas Brand Hollis, printed a mass of material, much of it free, in favour of parliamentary reform, at least 88,000 copies of thirty-three different publications in 1780–3.[19] The Society substantially supported the 1780 programme of the committee of the Westminster Association, including universal manhood suffrage, annual elections, the secret ballot and equal constituencies. The polarised and polarising nature of radical calls can be gauged from such titles as Cartwright's *The Legislative Rights of the Commonalty Vindicated; or Take Your Choice! Representation and Respect/Imposition and Contempt: Annual Parliaments and Liberty/Long Parliaments and Slavery* (1776). The French Revolution thus impacted on to a society that was far from static.

Notes

1   E. P. Thompson, *Customs in Common* (1992).

2   J. Innes, 'Politics, Property and the Middle Class', *Parliamentary History*, XI (1992), p. 291; J. R. Oldfield, 'The London Committee and mobilization of public opinion against the slave trade', *Historical Journal*, XXXV (1992), pp. 331–43.

3   J. E. Cookson, *The Friends of Peace: anti-war liberalism in England 1793–1815* (Cambridge, 1982), pp. 12–16; J. J. Sack, *From Jacobite to Conservative: reaction and orthodoxy in Britain, c. 1760–1832* (Cambridge, 1993), pp. 49–50.

4   R. Hole, *Pulpits, Politics and Public Order in England 1760–1832* (Cambridge, 1989); J. A. Phillips, *Electoral Behavior in Unreformed England* (Princeton, 1982); Bradley, *Popular Politics*, pp. 211–12; O'Gorman, *Voters, Patrons and Parties*, pp. 350–2, 359–68.

5   S. J. Connolly, *Religion, Law, and Power: the making of Protestant Ireland, 1660–1760* (Oxford, 1992); Smyth, *Men of No Property*.

6   A. M. Urdank, *Religion and Society in a Cotswold Vale: Nailsworth, Gloucestershire 1780–1865* (Berkeley, 1990), pp. 118, 125–6.

7   Black, *The English Press in the Eighteenth Century* (1987).

8   A. Aspinall, 'The reporting and publishing of the House of Commons debates 1771–1834', in R. Pares and A. J. P. Taylor eds., *Essays Presented to Sir Lewis Namier* (1956), pp. 227–57; Thomas, 'The beginning of parliamentary reporting in newspapers, 1768–1774', *English Historical Review*, LXXIV (1959), pp. 623–36; Lowe, 'Peers and Printers: the beginnings of sustained press coverage of the House of Lords in the 1770s', *Parliamentary History*, VII (1988), pp. 241–56.

9   P. Hyland, 'Liberty and libel: government and the press during the Succession Crisis in Britain, 1712–1716', *English Historical Review*, CI (1986), pp. 875–88.

10   Black, *English Press*, pp. 174–8

11   M. Harris, *London Newspapers in the Age of Walpole* (Cranbury, New Jersey, 1987).

12   Edmund Gibson to Bishop Nicolson of Derry, 11 April 1721, Bod. MS. A. 269 p. 97; J. P. Reid, *The Concept of Representation in the Age of the American Revolution* (Chicago, 1989).

13   A. P. W. Malcomson, 'A lost natural leader: John James Hamilton, First Marquess of Abercorn', *Proceedings of the Royal Irish Academy* LXXXVIII, C, no. 4 (1988), pp. 81–2; R. W. Davis, *Political Change and Continuity 1760–1885: a Buckinghamshire study* (Newton Abbot, 1972), p. 37.

14   Thorne ed., *The House of Commons* i, 4, 10, 43, 101.

15 Speck, 'Northumberland elections', p. 164.

16 M. J. Clark, 'The county community in Surrey 1774–1845' (D. Phil., Oxford, 1984), p. 461.

17 The extensive literature on radicalism can be approached through Dickinson, 'Radicals and reformers in the age of Wilkes and Wyvill', in Black ed., *British Politics and Society from Walpole to Pitt 1742–1789* (1990), pp. 123–46.

18 Colley, 'Eighteenth-century radicalism before Wilkes', *Transactions of the Royal Historical Society*, 5th ser. XXXI (1981), pp. 1–19; Dickinson, 'The precursors of political radicalism in Augustan Britain', in C. Jones ed., *Britain in the First Age of Party 1680–1750* (1987), pp. 63–84.

19 E. Royle and J. Walvin, *English Radicals and Reformers 1760–1848* (1982), p. 30.

6

The challenge of Revolution

The British response to the French Revolution, which broke out with the storming of the Bastille on 14 July 1789, reflected the strength and divisive role of ideological considerations. The Revolution and the response to it in Britain posed central questions about the nature of civil society and the legitimacy of the British system. If, in some respects, the politics of Britain, or, more particularly, England, had changed little between the 1690s and 1780s, the crisis of the 1790s was to pose new challenges not least in terms of new directions and urgency in ideological divisions and a more extensive public engagement in politics. The development of a language of class identity and interest was particularly notable.[1]

There was little difference along party lines in the reporting of the early stages of the Revolution by the British press.[2] This was largely because the Revolution, though seen as newsworthy, was not regarded as significant in terms of British politics. Debate over British political issues, and, in particular, the Dissenters' campaign for the repeal of the Test Act, was generally without reference to French developments.

There were, however, exceptions, and Edmund Burke did not originate the idea of using the Revolution as a means of condemning domestic developments that he disliked (Doc. 39). On 2 March 1790, a Commons debate on ? proposal for the repeal of the Test and Corporation Acts revealed the divisive nature of the issue. Opposition spokesmen publicly disagreed. Burke suggested that the Dissenting ministers were recommending the same attack on the Church as had happened in France. Fox, in contrast, praised the example of French moves towards toleration. The language of rights which played such a major role in French politics influenced the situation in Britain. Dissenters no longer sought repeal as a privilege and favour; they were proclaiming their rights. The *Daily Gazetteer*, a paper that supported parliamentary reform and repeal of the Test and Corporation Acts, favourably compared French changes with the British position in its issue of 12 January 1790.

Events in France, however, played little role in the general election of 1790, which was a major success for the government, despite the relative sophistication of opposition organisation.[3] A report in the *Ipswich Journal* of 21 August 1790 included the comment, 'I blushed to hear a gentleman . . . advert to France as an example of freedom, worthy of the imitation of the electors of Suffolk', but such comments appear to have been rare. The recent centenary of the Glorious Revolution played a larger role than the French Revolution in the election.

It was Burke's *Reflections on the Revolution in France, and on the Proceedings in Certain Societies in London relative to that event*, published on 1 November 1790, that made France a central topic of British political debate by linking developments in the two countries in a polemical fashion, and, by and in doing so, changed the nature of this political debate.[4] Burke's prominence, and the controversy that he aroused, led to wide discussion of his ideas. Conservatives naturally applauded: James, 2nd Earl of Fife thought the *Reflections* should be printed in gold, but others were also impressed. John Courtenay, a Foxite MP, sent a copy to his former patron, George, 1st Marquess Townshend, adding that it was 'universally read, and universally admired, as it well deserves to be, as the finest composition in the English language, and (bating a few exceptionable passages) inculcating the soundest constitutional doctrine, the true philosophy of human nature, and the best and purest morals'.[5]

The *Reflections* touched off a pamphlet debate, although the press was also of crucial importance, both in printing excerpts from the writings of Burke, his supporters and his critics, and in commenting upon them. Burke's analysis of *ancien régime* France was contested by his critics, but it was the progress of radical thought in Britain and the consequences of the Revolution for

British politics that aroused most interest. Radicalism created a sense of transience and vulnerability and this provoked the conscious statement of a conservative ideology, which was more than simply the formulation of views and assumptions that had earlier been substantially mute. Over the previous century the official ideology of Whiggism, if such a modern formulation can be used, had essentially argued that the Revolution Settlement had solved Britain's problems and created the best possible political system. Critics, however, had stressed mutability. They had argued that national character and institutions could alter as a result of social and political changes, such as the spread of corruption (Doc. 40). This was a central strand of Tory thought, its stress on the uncertainty of human affairs reflecting a distinct religious, moral and intellectual position in which the power of human calculation, and thus the stability of human institutions, were minimised (Doc. 41).

During the early eighteenth century, opposition writers, some of them radical Whigs, argued that Britain could readily follow the example of the Continental states that had a more autocratic political system, and that the Revolution Settlement had failed to safeguard Britain against despotism, because no event or constitution could preclude the consequences of misrule and corruption. The Continent was presented as a stage depicting what would happen to Britain were it to be misgoverned; the price of liberty was therefore eternal vigilance.[6]

When change came in France in 1789, it became for conservative British commentators a stage depicting what could happen to the country were it run by the opposition, or, even more worryingly, by their radical allies, such as Tom Paine, who offered an alternative model of political order. On 30 January 1793 Samuel Horsley, Bishop of St Davids, preached the annual commemorative sermon for the execution of Charles I in 1649. This was seen as a martyrdom, the most significant episode in the post-Reformation history of the Church of England. Horsley's sermon, delivered in the immediate aftermath of the execution of Louis XVI, served to reaffirm the political theory of Anglican high-churchmanship and to associate it with hostility to revolution. Horsley himself was a follower of Pitt who in 1789 had urged his diocesan clergy in Carmarthen to oppose the Foxite John Philipps at the forthcoming general election because

Philipps had voted for the repeal of the Test and Corporation Acts in 1787.[7] Burke followed a long line of clerical analysis of Christian culture.

Conversely, opposition writers were driven to defend their cause, and, by extension, the situation in France. Paine's *The Rights of Man* (1791–2) was a widely-read reply to Burke's *Reflections*, which comfortably outsold it, and, in part two, went well beyond responding to Burke by offering a radical *social* programme. What worried government was that Paine offered an alternative social as well as an alternative political order, one in which there was little room for nobility, established Church and monarchy.[8] Under the stimulus of the *Reflections*, opinions about the Revolution and its implications became more defined, a process encouraged by the extent to which Burke's attitude provided ministerial writers with a valuable opportunity to divide the opposition. In addition, the determination of radicals to organise and proselytise underlined Burke's insistence that the cause of revolution was indeed universal in its intentions and threat, though he failed to draw attention to the differences between indigenous and French radicalism.

The Revolutionary and Napoleonic period witnessed both a renewal of the ideological themes of the British *ancien régime* and the birth of modern British conservatism with its scepticism about the possibilities of secular improvement and its stress on historical continuity and national values, rather than present-mindedness and internationalism, or the alternative modern impetus behind British conservatism, the furtherance of capitalism and the concomitant defence of certain sectional interests. This Burkean conservatism was not necessarily restricted to Britain: Burke himself treated pre-Revolutionary Europe as a community and a commonwealth, was very concerned about the situation in France and was averse to any peace with her that did not entail a counter-revolution. A stress on continuity and, therefore, the value of specific constitutional and political inheritances, however, did not readily lend itself to serving as the basis of an international ideology. Despite Burke's polemic about a European community being assaulted by the French Revolution, and, earlier, by the powers that had partitioned much of Poland in 1772, the appeal to history (continuity) against reason (intellectual arguments for change) was inherently nationalist.[9] Indeed, one of the major intellectual problems facing the forces of conservatism or, as they later became, the 'right' in Europe, during the Enlightenment, the Revolutionary–Napoleonic period and subsequently, was the difficulty in formulating and sustaining an international ideology. The variegated nature of the *ancien régime*, with its religious divisions and its latent or patent ideology of specific privileges, did not lend itself to this task, no more than did the xenophobic, provincial, proto-nationalist and nationalist European responses to French power in 1792–1815.

Burke was depressed by the unwillingness of the British government to act against revolutionary France and British radicalism (Doc. 42), but, once the French had successfully resisted a Austrian-supported Prussian invasion in September 1792 and then gone on that November to conquer the Austrian Netherlands (modern Belgium) and to threaten Britain's major ally, the United Provinces (Netherlands), the situation dramatically altered. Reports reaching the government from around Britain spoke of a rising tide of agitation, before which the local authorities often felt helpless.[10] Some of the leading Whigs were so concerned that they were willing to offer the government support in 'strong measures' and there was interest in Whig ranks in a coalition designed to produce unity against radicalism.[11] The Foreign Secretary, William, Lord Grenville, echoed the governmental response to both Jacobitism and the American War of Independence, when rebellion and French intervention were seen as mutually-supporting threats, by suggesting that there was 'a concerted plan to drive us to extremities, with a view of producing an impression in the interior of the country'.[12] In 1792, a poor harvest was steadily working through into higher prices and this was leading to rising social discontent, much as rising food prices had done in France in the summer of 1789. Much discontent in Britain in 1792 was not politically specific, but some was, and the spread of radical agitation led to concern at every point.[13] Radical political clubs, such as the Sheffield Society for Constitutional Information founded in 1791 and the London Corresponding Society launched the following year, were growing in size and prominence, and some were in touch with the French assemblies.[14] Congratulatory addresses, applauding the Convention's policies, were dispatched prominently.[15] Such radical activities reflected a perception, shared with Burke, that events in France were of direct relevance to Britain.

None of the means or media of public politics employed by the radicals in late 1792 was new, but they were alarming for three reasons. First, they were definitely focused on non-parliamentary, rather than parliamentary, action, and thus represented a rejection of existing constitutional mechanisms. Secondly, they were focused on a foreign power, France, the traditional national enemy, a formidable military force that had beaten Britain in the last war and was currently demonstrating its military strength. Thirdly, the very volatility of international, especially French, developments made the situation in Britain appear more precarious.

Discontent and agitation were not restricted to England; much of Scotland and Ireland appeared unstable. Concern about the views of Irish Catholics led to their being given the vote in 1793, a measure forced on the Dublin Castle administration by the British government. The King's Birthday Riot in Edinburgh in June 1792 was directed against the government, there were fresh riots that November, especially in Dundee, and on 11 December 1792 the first national convention of the radical Scottish Friends of the People, an association launched that July, opened in Edinburgh.[16] The British army was too small to cope with insurrection, defend Britain from invasion and campaign in the Low Countries. When such a strategy had been last tried, in 1745–6, it had proved necessary both to bring back most of the army from the Low Countries and to send for Dutch and Hessian forces. Concerned about the situation in England in late 1792, George III refused to send any troops thence to Ireland.[17] In response to the threat of insurrection,[18] the government moved troops nearer to London and on 1 December called up part of the militia, a step that obliged it to summon Parliament within a fortnight. The manner in which Parliament was not formulating policy, but played a central role in its verification and legitimation, was indicative of the nature of parliamentary government.

The ministry was to be helped by the rapid development of loyalism, the rallying to Church, Crown and nation, in reaction to the atheism, republicanism and success of Revolutionary France, that was such an obvious feature of Europe from 1791: counter-revolution as popular action and even revolution. Loyalism was a genuine mass movement, especially in England;[19]

even if it proved difficult to sustain the level of engagement, there were many not comprehended within it, and the relationship between government and Loyalism could be ambiguous. Much of the press was harnessed to spread a message of loyalty and order (Doc. 43). The ideological conflict helped to broaden the political base. The mixture of national identity, economic interest, religious conviction and a 'sense of security' was to prove a very potent message. Ideology, an appeal to the interests, in every sense, of the propertied, appeared preferable and more advisable than a reliance on force. On 20 November 1792 the Association for Preserving Liberty and Property against Republicans and Levellers was launched at a meeting at the Crown and Anchor Tavern in London (Doc. 44). It has been claimed that about 1,500 loyalist associations, involving about 15,000 active members, were formed between November 1792 and February 1793.[20] The development of bellicose loyalism and conservatism was encouraged by the ministry, though far from dependent on its support. James Bland Burges, Under Secretary at the Foreign Office, played an active role in the foundation of the *True Briton* and *Sun*. A clear effort was made to marginalise radicals and to suggest that the nation was united behind the government (Doc. 45).

The *True Briton* was launched in January 1793 on the presses of the *Argus*, a radical London paper that had been brought to an end the previous year: its printer Sampson Perry was outlawed when he fled to France to avoid trial for libel. Action against opposition publications was more than episodic. The printer and editor of the *Morning Chronicle* were tried and acquitted of seditious libel in 1793, the year in which the *Leicester Chronicle* and the *Manchester Herald* ended as a result of government action. Daniel Holt, the printer of the former, was convicted of seditious libel and sent to Newgate Prison. Thereafter, there was a marked slackening in action, though that did not save the *Sheffield Register* in 1794 or prevent the imprisonment of James Montgomery, the conductor of the radical *Sheffield Iris* for political libels in 1795 and 1796.[21] Prosecutions of radicals at the local level were effective, notably in Birmingham, Manchester and Sheffield. Plans for a national convention of radicals for London were disrupted by the arrest of the leaders of the reform societies on 12 May 1794. That year *Habeas Corpus* (the requirement to produce a person before a court and thus prevention of imprisonment without trial) was suspended. In 1795 the Treasonable Practices Act made serious criticism of the king, the government or the constitution a treasonable practice. The Seditious Meetings Act, also of 1795, sought to block the recourse to mass meetings, which had been used with some effect by the radicals. These measures definitely hindered the radical societies. The membership of the London Corresponding Society declined. Most of the leadership of the relatively numerous Sheffield radicals had fled or been prosecuted by 1796. Clandestine activity, however, continued, though there is controversy over its significance and over the possibility of revolution at the end of the 1790s and in the early 1800s.

It is important to dwell on the press, because the government's sometimes rigorous use of its repressive powers has been discussed as an aspect of state terror,[22] and the fate of the press can serve as a ready litmus test; indeed is generally used thus in the discussion of modern political systems. First, it is significant that radical opinions were still expressed in the press, for example, by the *Bury and Norwich Post* and the *Cambridge Intelligencer*,[23] and several London papers, most obviously the *Morning Chronicle*, bitterly criticised government policy, although the country was involved from 1793 in a war that became increasingly hazardous. Secondly, at least one important proposal for systematic government action, John Adolphus's 1799 plan for a regulating office, was not followed up,[24] though in 1798 new legislation compelled the recording of the names and addresses of printers and publishers on every copy of a paper, prohibited the export of papers to enemy states and closed the oft-used loophole of permitting foreign newspapers to serve as a source for opposition reports; and a registration of printing presses was introduced in 1799. Adolphus's proposal is interesting, first because it reveals the extent to which the critical situation of the 1790s, defeat abroad and radicalism at home, led to the airing of new views on the regulation of the press, and secondly because the episode demonstrates the relatively cautious response of the Pitt ministry. In contrast, at least one-sixth of the journalists known to have been active in Paris in 1790–1 were executed in the Revolutionary Terror of 1793–4.[25] There was no reign of terror in Britain and the government took few initiatives. It provided no support in 1799 for Lord Belgrave's motion for the suppression of Sunday papers. Six years earlier, no action was taken on the suggestion that the ministry purchase the *Birmingham and Stafford Chronicle* in order to prevent a possible acquisition by radicals.[26]

Clearly the ministry could live with a degree of criticism from a legal press that was greater than was commonly the case in Europe. The cause for that has to be sought not in the British press of the period, but in British history, specifically political culture. The ability of the British state to respond to the Revolutionary–Napoleonic crisis, but yet to do so within existing forms, and in part to reflect their strengths and limitations, was an accentuation of a more general feature of the state in the late eighteenth century, its flexibility. Though it had been far from static, the Old Corps Whig government of the Walpole–Pelham period is, rightly, not generally associated with reform. Indeed there was a defensive character to government then, a concern to avoid crisis, political, Jacobite or international, often apparently to the exclusion of much else. By the time of the ministry of Pitt the Younger, however, the concern with public finance and imperial regulation that had played such a major role in government from 1763 on had broadened out into a more general conscious acceptance of reform. This was designed to produce effective administration, to support and foster a system capable of peaceful change and economic growth.

Though the Revolutionary period was a serious challenge to the assumptions of the political élite, not least in the creation of a language of class conflict, this challenge was faced with, outside Ireland, limited civil disorder, and with a major stress on the use of traditional methods. Indeed, the very conservatism of the response to Revolution, and the stress on continuity, precedent, privilege and law as (with the crucial addition of religion) the ideological focus of nationhood and counter-Revolution, ensured that the development of new practices, institutions, ideas and notions took place within a context in which their implications for change were not probed, while their novelty was understated. Britain was not apart from the process by which, in response to the strain of war, states as diverse as Prussia and Turkey improved the effectiveness of government in the Revolutionary–Napoleonic period, and crisis brought a new intensity and focus to the ideological context of British political activity, national identity and, in large part, cultural and intellectual life. In Britain, however, the undoubted stresses of these years did not lead to the abandonment of the past. Parliamentary government survived. Although its scope was not comprehensive, the savageries displayed in the suppression of the Irish rising of 1798 being especially notable, the rule of law continued. Indeed there were some conspicuous defeats for the ministry. The association of political reform with the opposition became far more marked, and thus helped to thwart it. Whereas Pitt could support parliamentary reform in 1785, Charles Grey's motions in 1793 and 1797 were defeated on Commons divisions of 282–41 and 256–91. A major effect of the French Revolution on British politics was to retard parliamentary reform.

A modern parallel is instructive, not least because it warns against the habit of adopting a linear approach to history, and, instead, suggests the possibility of a 'structural' emphasis. Though there were threats of insurrection[27] and invasion,[28] Britain survived the Revolutionary–Napoleonic period without occupation and the transforming changes that total defeat brought elsewhere. In the Second World War, Britain was similarly badly hurt, but not conquered. Thanks to her insular position, her geopolitical situation – both in and yet also outside Europe – she had thus repeated the experience of the Revolutionary–Napoleonic period. This helped to ensure that Britain followed a different political trajectory in the postwar world from that of her Continental neighbours. Throughout the Continent, right-wing parties and tendencies had been discredited, thanks to their association with Fascism and collaboration, ensuring that they would be reborn in the form of Christian Democracy, a tradition different from that of British conservatism; while, within the left, the role of the Communists in resistance movements gave them greater weight and thus helped to sustain a division between Socialism and Communism that was of limited consequence in Britain. The disastrous experience of war and occupation also lent energy to the idea of European union, to the willingness to surrender some of the powers and prerogatives of the nation state to supra-national bodies. This was easier for societies undergoing considerable change and whose political structures were being transformed (as those of France, Germany and Italy were in 1944–58), than for Britain. Similarly, the political structure of Japan was greatly altered during the American occupation of 1945–52. Thus, alongside the more usual point that it was the economies badly damaged in the war (Japan and Germany especially, France and Italy to a lesser extent) that did best in the postwar world, it was also the case that these were states that were defeated and that experienced political and institutional change, while the victors (the Soviet Union, the USA and Britain) essentially maintained their political structures.

It was this factor that was crucial to the nineteenth-century British state: the experience of the Revolutionary–Napoleonic crisis did not alter fundamentally the British state, the major exception being the Act of Union with Ireland in 1800. This dissolved the separate Irish Parliament in return for Irish representation at Westminster: the Commons had to be enlarged to accommodate a hundred new MPs. Like the 1707 Union with Scotland, Union with Ireland was a response to the danger of divergence from the wishes of politicians in London, specifically a fear that Britain would be weakened in her conflict with France by an unstable Ireland (Doc. 46). Rising Catholic wealth and divisions among the Protestants were important to the long-term process by which the Catholics came to play a more central role in politics. The enormous expansion in Catholic recruitment during the Revolutionary and Napoleonic wars had a significant bearing on the process of politicisation. Important initiatives to improve their legal position were, however, blocked. Earl Fitzwilliam, Lord Lieutenant 1794–5, sought to remove the legal disabilities affecting Irish Catholics but was disavowed and recalled. Pitt's attempt to follow Union by Catholic emancipation was thwarted. Fitzwilliam had believed that concessions were necessary in order to block the spread of Jacobinism (revolutionary activity on the French model), and his failure helped in the alienation of Irish Catholic opinion. The United Irishmen had already begun to plot revolution, but Fitzwilliam's failure contributed to a sense that there was no political solution to the rising sectarian violence that was to culminate in rebellion in 1798. More people were killed in Ireland that year than during the whole of the Terror in France. This rebellion demonstrated that the Ascendancy could not keep Ireland stable, and encouraged the British government to support Union.[29]

The Union was to have a major effect on nineteenth-century British politics, but, with this important exception, the striking feature is one of continuity. This is a marked contrast to France, Spain, Italy, Germany, Poland, the Low Countries and Scandinavia, and helps to explain why the historical importance to Britain of the eighteenth century should not be underrated. As already suggested, geopolitics, specifically the combination of Britain's insular position and her role as the strongest maritime power in the world, were in part responsible for the country's distinctive trajectory, but it is also important to consider how much should be attributed to the nature of the British political system.

The inability of the British state to absorb imperial tensions had been demonstrated in relations with the Thirteen Colonies in the 1770s, but the kingdom had proved more resilient in dealing with domestic tensions, including the challenging experience of defeat and loss of empire, in the 1780s. Close attention to the early 1780s, however, suggests a less optimistic conclusion, and it is clear both then, and a decade later, that critics of the system were prepared to turn to novel and extra-parliamentary political means. A clear sense of crisis, current or imminent, emerges from much of the political correspondence of these years and it can be seen in the letters of politicians with very different ideas (Docs 47, 48). The crisis in relations between George III and the Fox–North ministry created a serious political situation, and its resolution in the form of a Pitt ministry enjoying backing in Parliament was far from inevitable. Yet, once Crown–élite consensus had been restored, at least in so far as was measured by the ability of George III to co-operate with a ministry enjoying the support of Parliament, Britain was politically stable. Unlike during the period of the Jacobite challenge, this was not a question of ministerial stability but more general political instability, at least that is until the rise of domestic radicalism in the early 1790s altered the situation by ensuring that the support of Parliament was not sufficient to produce political stability. This was recognised by the government's efforts to sponsor loyalism from 1792 on.

Prior to the Revolutionary crisis, there was a considerable measure of stability, and that was not disturbed either by the failure to introduce parliamentary reform or by the measures of the Pitt ministry. A stable and relatively united government enjoying a considerable measure of public support, therefore, faced the crisis from 1792, an obvious contrast with the situation in France. The parliamentary system brought a considerable measure of élite consensus in Britain: if not necessarily support for government and its policies, then at least acceptance of its position. In contrast to the position under Walpole, when the Revolution Settlement was still being defined and debated, and constitutional and political conventions were being established, the situation was arguably more stable by the 1780s, though the controversy over George III's conduct in 1783–4 and that over the nature of a regency government in 1788–9[30] were reminders that conventions and their application were far from fixed (Doc. 49). This consensus was to hold firm in 1792–4, as most of the élite lined up behind the ministry, many abandoning the Whig party,[31] which, under Fox, became an ineffective rump for the remainder of the decade.[32] Indeed, after the failure of Grey's motion for parliamentary reform on 26 May 1797, Fox and his followers seceded from the Commons and most remained away until Pitt fell in 1801.

In France, in contrast, in the late 1780s and early 1790s, there was no time to establish widely-acceptable constitutional conventions, and the élite was fatally fractured, successive divisions between Louis XVI and a series of assemblies undermining the chances of securing any lasting agreement. The revolutionary consequences justified some of Burke's concern about the results both of a desire for major changes and of élite division. Thus, the constitutional and political differences between the two states, Britain and France, proved more important in this period than the similarities between the two societies.

Yet, it would be inappropriate to close on a comforting note that replaces the teleology of Whig progress by the inevitability of 'structural' features, specifically the nature of the political system, and crucially the attitudes that constituted the political culture of the period. Such an interpretation does violence to the doubts, fears and uncertainties of contemporaries, and ignores the nature of the contingent, both before the Revolutionary crisis and during it. Alarming as the early 1780s, both the general sense of crisis and, more specifically, the several, but very different, crises of 1780, 1782 and 1783–4, were to most contemporary commentators, it was and is possible to sketch out various political scenarios that would have led then to a more serious or more lasting crisis.

A sense of crisis had re-emerged in late 1788, as a result of the serious and surprising breakdown of George III's health. His eldest son, George, Prince of Wales, was no friend to his father or his ministers, and thus the question mark that the reversionary interest posed against the policies and personnel of the governments in all the monarchies of the period (Doc. 50) was dramatically highlighted in Britain in 1788. It had been a serious problem for the governments of both George I and George II, most obviously in 1717–20 and 1747–51, when their respective heirs had led opposition to them. The abrupt and sweeping differences that a new monarch could make had been demonstrated with the fall of the Tories after the accession of George I, and again when George III himself had succeeded to the throne in 1760. That had been followed by a striking demonstration of the continued political importance of the monarch, and thus of the potential volatility of the system, its dependence on the views, health and life of one man. George III's accession had led to the fall of Pitt (1761) and Newcastle (1762), the end of the Old Corps Whig system, the reintegration of the Tories into national political life and a decisive break with Continental interventionism and the alliance with Prussia.

It was scarcely surprising that the reversionary interest posed a question mark against ministerial stability, as in August 1786, when the deranged Margaret Nicholson tried to kill George III (Doc. 51), or in late 1788 when it was assumed that as soon as the Prince of Wales became Regent he would dismiss the government and ask Fox to form a new one. In 1784 George, 16th Earl of Morton wrote of George III and Pitt, 'the existence of Ministry depends on his and one other life, either of which failing, the whole would fall to the ground. The same may be said of opposition.' 'Can anything describe the violence of the present times . . . ?', asked James, 2nd Earl of Fife of the parliamentary debates of December 1788.[33]

Long-term trends were to lessen the role of the monarchy, and that despite George III's growing popularity from the 1783–4 crisis on. The growth of business and the increased scope of government lessened the ability of one man, whether monarch or minister, to master the situation. This helped to encourage the development of the Cabinet. The ministries of Pitt the Younger and Lord Liverpool were especially important in this process. The discussions and decisions of the inner core of ministers, the Cabinet council, became more formal. Collective responsibility and loyalty to the leading minister increased, and this strengthened the Cabinet's ties with that minister and increased his power with reference to the monarch. Royal influence and patronage declined with the abolition of sinecures, the diminishing influence of Court favourites and the growing accountability of Parliament.

Nevertheless, the extent and impact of these processes in the 1780s should not be exaggerated. Personal factors were to be very important: the illness of George III in 1788–9, the subsequent slackening of his grasp and his later illnesses; the lack of interest displayed by George IV; the impact of Pitt's longevity in office. These still, however, lay in the future. Greater Cabinet cohesion and influence and consistent united Cabinet control of policy-making, were more a feature of the 1790s than of the 1780s.[34]

The reversionary interest and the Regency Crisis were the most dramatic cause and episode of doubt about governmental instability in the period from the 1784 general election to the Revolutionary crisis, but there was also awareness of serious ministerial divisions, most significantly between Pitt and Lord Thurlow, Lord Chancellor, Leader of the House of Lords, and the minister closest to the king. This division was linked to policy, as Thurlow was more conservative than Pitt over, for example, parliamentary reform and the suppression of the slave trade (Doc. 52). Pitt was to resign in 1801 because George III did not share his support for Catholic emancipation.[35]

Thus an element of the contingent was present in this period, despite ministerial successes in the 1784 and 1790 elections, and the weakness of the opposition. This element was more obvious once war with Revolutionary France had broken out as defeat in war and economic problems at home posed a significant challenge to Loyalism. The extent and nature of radicalism in the late 1790s are difficult to discern and have led to controversy, but it is clear that the naval mutinies of 1797 were a serious challenge to the government, though specific grievances arising from pay and conditions were principally at stake. Labour disputes were a major feature of the decade, especially in 1791–2, and in 1795. Harvest failures led to serious food rioting in 1795–6 and 1800–1.[36] Similarly, Wellington's successes in the Peninsular War in Spain and Portugal (1808–13) were accompanied by serious economic and social strains in Britain, including Luddite violence against new technology and other aspects of violent industrial protest. These strains became more intense in the late 1810s as a result of postwar economic depression. However, the Liverpool government's reconstruction of 1822 reaffirmed the resilience of the political system and its ability to absorb social, economic and political pressures, though the situation was also eased by the prosperity of the early 1820s.

The apparent certainties of structural analysis, whether geopolitical or political–cultural, thus dissolve under scrutiny. Instead, it is possible to emphasise what would have been most apparent to contemporaries, the complex nature of the political system and the element of chance.

Notes

1 M. Butler, *Burke, Paine, Godwin and the Revolution Controversy* (Cambridge, 1984); G. Claeys, 'The French Revolution and British political thought', *History of Political Thought*, XI (1990), pp. 59–80.

2 Black, 'The British press and the French Revolution', in M. Vovelle ed., *La Revolution française* (4 vols, Paris, 1989), i, 371–9, and 'The British press and eighteenth-century revolution: the French case', in P. Dukes and J. Dunkley eds., *Culture and Revolution* (1990), pp. 110–20.

3 D. E. Ginter, *Whig Organization in the General Election of 1790* (Berkeley, 1967).

4 The literature on Burke, the *Reflections* and the subsequent controversy is vast. F. P. Lock, *Burke's Reflections on the Revolution in France* (1985) and S. Blakemore ed., *Burke and the French Revolution* (Athens, Georgia, 1992) are good recent introductions. The best recent edition is in L. G. Mitchell ed., *The Writings and Speeches of Edmund Burke. 8: 1790–1794* (Oxford, 1989), while the best guide to the works produced in the controversy is G. T. Pendelton, 'Towards a bibliography of the *Reflections* and *Rights of Man* controversy', *Bulletin of Research in the Humanities*, LXXXV (1982), pp. 65–103. A crucial topic is covered in J. T. Boulton, *The Language of Politics in the Age of Wilkes and Burke* (1963). Pendelton, 'The English pamphlet literature of the age of the French

Revolution anatomized', *Eighteenth-Century Life*, V (1978), pp. 29–37; and M. Butler, *Burke, Paine, Godwin and the Revolution Controversy* (Cambridge, 1984) are valuable.

5   Fife to William Rose, 25, 27 November, 3 December 1790, 4 January 1791, Aberdeen, University Library 2226/131; Courtenay to Townshend, 4 November 1790, New Haven, Beinecke Library, Osborn Shelves, Townshend Box 5.

6   Dickinson, *Liberty and Property*; Browning, *Political and Constitutional Ideas of the Court Whigs* (Baton Rouge, 1982); Black, 'Ideology, history, xenophobia and the world of print in eighteenth-century England', in Black and Gregory eds., *Culture, Politics and Society*, pp. 184–216.

7   Hole, *Pulpits*, pp. 160–73; F. C. Mather, *High Church Prophet: Bishop Samuel Horsley (1733–1806) and the Caroline tradition in the later Georgian Church* (Oxford, 1992), pp. 71–6, 228–9.

8   B. Kuklick ed., *Paine: political writings* (Cambridge, 1989), pp. 49–203.

9   T. P. Schofield, 'Conservative political thought in Britain in response to the French Revolution', *Historical Journal*, XXIX (1986), pp. 601–22; J. Dinwiddy, 'England', in O. Dann and Dinwiddy eds., *Nationalism in the Age of the French Revolution* (1988), pp. 53–70; G. L. Vincitorio, 'Burke and the partition of Poland', in Vincitorio ed., *Crisis in the 'Great Republic'* (New York, 1969), pp. 33–42.

10   T. C. W. Blanning, *The Origins of the French Revolutionary Wars* (Harlow, 1986), pp. 131–59; Pitt to Lord Grenville, Foreign Secretary, [11 November 1792], BL. Add. 58906 fos 144–5.

11   Duke of Portland, head of the Whig party in the Lords, to Earl of Malmesbury, 21 October, Earl of Darnley to Malmesbury, 21 October, Viscount Palmerston to Malmesbury, 9 October 1792, Winchester, Hampshire CRO. Malmesbury papers vols. 179, 149, 162; William Windham to Thomas Grenville, 14 November 1792, Bod. MS. Eng. Lett. c. 144 fo. 306.

12   Grenville to William, Lord Auckland, Ambassador in The Hague, 27 November 1792, BL. Add. 34445 fo. 401.

13   Ehrman's chapter '1792: the dimensions of unrest', *Pitt* ii, 91–171, is an excellent introduction to this subject.

14   A. W. L. Seaman, 'Reform politics at Sheffield, 1791–97', *Transactions of the Hunter Archaeological Society*, VII (1957), pp. 215–28; C. Jewson, *Jacobin City: a portrait of Norwich in its reaction to the French Revolution, 1788–1802* (Edinburgh, 1975); A. Goodwin, *The Friends of Liberty: the English democratic movement in the age of the French Revolution* (1979); E. Royle and J. Walvin, *British Radicals and Reformers 1760–1848*

(Brighton, 1982); M. Thale ed., *Selections from the Papers of the London Corresponding Society 1792–1799* (Cambridge, 1983); Dickinson, *British Radicalism and the French Revolution 1789–1815* (Oxford, 1985); Stevenson, 'The "Friends of France": the English provinces and the French Revolution 1789–93', *Franco-British Studies*, VI (1988), pp. 61–70; Claeys, *Thomas Paine: social and political thought* (1989).

15   Goodwin, *Friends of Liberty*, pp. 241–62, 507–14.

16   J. Brims, 'From reformers to "Jacobins": The Scottish Association of the Friends of the People', in T. M. Devine ed., *Conflict and Stability in Scottish Society 1700–1850* (Edinburgh, 1990), pp. 31–40; E. O'Flaherty, 'The Catholic Convention and Anglo-Irish politics 1791–93', *Archivium Hibernicum*, XL (1985), pp. 14–34; D. W. Miller, ed., *Peep O'Day Boys and Defenders: selected documents on the disturbances in County Armagh, 1784–1796* (Belfast, 1990); C. J. Woods ed., *Journals and Memoirs of Thomas Russell* (Blackrock, 1992).

17   George III to Grenville, 26 November 1792, BL. Add. 58857 fo. 62.

18   James Bland Burges, Under-Secretary at the Foreign Office, to Grenville, 4 November 1792, BL. Add. 58968 fol. 72; C. Emsley, 'The London "Insurrection" of December 1792: fact, fiction, or fantasy', *Journal of British Studies*, XVII (1978), pp. 66–86.

19   D. M. G. Sutherland, *France 1789–1815: revolution and counter-revolution* (1985), esp. pp. 14, 107–14; J. R. Western, 'The volunteer movement as an anti-revolutionary force, 1793–1802', *English Historical Review*, LXXI (1956), pp. 603–14; R. B. Rose, 'The Priestley Riots of 1791', *Past and Present*, XVIII (1960), pp. 68–88; A. Mitchell, 'The association movement of 1792–3', *Historical Journal*, IV (1961), pp. 56–77; Ginter, 'The loyalist association movement of 1792–3 and British public opinion', *Historical Journal*, IX (1966), pp. 179–90; R. R. Dozier, *For King, Constitution and Country: the English Loyalists and the French Revolution* (Lexington, 1983); A. Booth, 'Popular Loyalism and public violence in the north-west of England 1790–1800', *Social History*, VIII (1983), pp. 295–313; Cookson, 'The English volunteer movement of the French Wars, 1793–1815: some contexts', *Historical Journal*, XXXII (1989), pp. 867–91; Dickinson, 'Popular loyalism in Britain in the 1790s', in E. Hellmuth ed., *The Transformation of Political Culture. England and Germany in the late eighteenth century* (Oxford, 1990), pp. 503–33; D. Eastwood, 'Patriotism and the English state in the 1790s', in M. Philp ed., *The French Revolution and British Popular Politics* (Cambridge, 1991), pp. 146–68; Colley, *Britons* (New Haven, 1992), pp. 283–319.

20   Dozier, *For King*, p. 62.

21   T. M. Blagg, *Newark as a Publishing Town* (Newark, 1898), p. 57;

W. H. G. Armytage, 'The editorial experiences of Joseph Gales', *North Carolina Historical Review*, XXVIII (1951), pp. 332–61; D. Read, *Press and People 1790–1850: opinion in three English cities* (1961), pp. 69–73; J. Wigley, 'James Montgomery and the *Sheffield Iris*, 1792–1825: A study in the weakness of provincial radicalism', *Transactions of the Hunter Archaeological Society*, X (1975), pp. 173–81.

22 R. R. Rea, '"The liberty of the press" as an issue in English politics, 1792–1793', *The Historian*, XXIV (1961), pp. 26–43; F. K. Prochaska, 'English state trials in the 1790s: a case study', *Journal of British Studies*, XIII (1973), pp. 63–82; Pendleton, 'Radicalism and the English 'Reign of Terror': the evidence of the pamphlet literature', *Proceedings of the Consortium on Revolutionary Europe* (1979); Emsley, 'An aspect of Pitt's 'Terror': prosecutions for sedition during the 1790s', *Social History*, VI (1981), pp. 155–84, and 'Repression, "Terror" and the rule of law in England during the decade of the French Revolution', *English Historical Review*, C (1985), pp. 801–25; J. Barrell, *The Birth of Pandora and the Division of Knowledge* (1992), pp. 119–43.

23 M. J. Murphy, 'Newspapers and opinion in Cambridge, 1780–1850', *Transactions of the Cambridge Bibliographical Society*, VI (1972), p. 41.

24 Adolphus to William Windham, 25 March 1799, BL. Add. 37878 fos 82–5.

25 J. Popkin, *Revolutionary News: the press in France 1789–1799* (Durham, North Carolina, 1990), pp. 53–4.

26 Cobbett, *Parliamentary History*, XXXIV, p. 1006; Money, *Experience and Identity*, p. 62; Christie, *Myth and Reality in Late-Eighteenth-Century British Politics and Other Papers* (1970), p. 328.

27 R. Wells, *Insurrection: the British experience, 1795–1803* (Gloucester, 1983), and 'Britain's avoidance of revolution in the 1790s revisited', *Bulletin of the Society for the Study of Labour History*, LIV (1989) and 'English society and revolutionary politics in the 1790s: the case for insurrection', in Philp ed., *Revolution*, pp. 188–226.

28 R. Glover, *Britain at Bay: defence against Bonaparte, 1803–14* (1973).

29 G. C. Bolton, *The Passing of the Irish Act of Union: a study in parliamentary politics* (1966); J. Smyth, *The Men of No Property: Irish radicals and popular politics in the late eighteenth century* (1992); T. Bartlett, *The Fall and Rise of the Irish Nation: the Catholic Question 1690–1830* (Dublin, 1992), pp. 244–67; R. B. McDow ll, 'The Fitzwilliam episode', *Irish Historical Studies*, XV (1966), pp. 115–30.

30 Derry, *The Regency Crisis and the Whigs 1788–9* (Cambridge, 1963).

31   Mitchell, *Charles James Fox and the Disintegration of the Whig Party 1782–1794* (Oxford, 1971), pp. 194–238.

32   Mitchell, *Charles James Fox* (Oxford, 1992), pp. 132–67.

33   Morton to Keith, 13 July 1784, BL. Add. 35532 fo. 140; Fife to William Rose, 16 Dec. 1788, Aberdeen, University Library, 2226/131.

34   Aspinall, 'The Cabinet Council 1783–1835', *Proceedings of the British Academy*, XXXVIII (1952), pp. 145–252 is largely devoted to the early nineteenth century; R. Pares, *King George III and the Politicians* (Oxford, 1953), pp. 143–81; Ehrman, *Pitt*, i, 180–6, 628–35; Christie, 'The Cabinet in the reign of George III, to 1790', in Christie, *Myth and Reality* (1970), pp. 58–108; C. Middleton, 'The impact of the American and French Revolutions on the British constitution: a case study of the British Cabinet', *Consortium on Revolutionary Europe Proceedings 1986*, pp. 317–26.

35   P. Mackesy, *War without Victory: the downfall of Pitt 1799–1802* (Oxford, 1984), pp. 195–201.

36   J. Bohstedt, *Riots and Community Politics in England and Wales, 1790–1810* (Cambridge, Mass., 1983).

Selected documents

Document 1

Establishment propaganda at a time of war with France. Richard Tucker (Weymouth) to John Tucker MP, 10 March 1744 Bod. MS. Don. c. 107 fos 17–18.

Mr. Clark the Judge who gave the charge I believe had studied good part of it, which was visibly calculated to work upon the passions of his auditors: – there was a great deal said of the excellency of our religion laws and government and a long encomium upon the former branch and then much of the lenity of our government touching Roman Catholics whom though our laws do not permit to enjoy the use of their religion yet the connivance of the government has been almost equal to the toleration allowed by law to Protestant Dissenters and therefore it is the more extraordinary that any of them should ever think of disturbing the peace of a government so indulgent but it is notorious to all the world and he was not afraid to say that it had ever been the restless principle of France to promote and encourage factions here as well as in all the countries in Europe to carry on their own perfidious schemes . . . he expatiated upon the excellency of our government when compared with any of the neighbouring powers . . . as the family [Stuarts] have been supported and bred up at the charity of France and nursed in the politics of that country they will be under such obligations there that this nation must become a province of France.

Document 2

The influence of the landed notables: the Northumberland by-election of 1786. Two letters to the Duke of Northumberland, first from William Charleton, of 11 June reporting what Sir Charles Grey was told when canvassing, the second from John Blackett, of 12 June, reporting a response to canvassing on behalf of John Trevelyan. Alnwick Castle, Y.v.I.d.

> I am perfectly sensible that the principal gentlemen in this county will know who His Grace the Duke of Northumberland wishes to patronize before they give their votes for anyone.

> . . . he would answer Trevelyan, that he thought the Duke intitled to *one* member, that his late father's opposition in 1774 arose from no public or private pique to the late Duke but from an idea instilled into him, that the Duke wanted both members . . .

Document 3

The fall of Walpole was followed by pressure for a change in the system and practice of government. John Campbell of Cawdor MP, a Lord of the Admiralty under Walpole, was suspicious of the opposition Whigs now rising to power, such as William Pulteney, and linked public opinion, of which he was critical, to a lack of self-control on the part of those that had aroused it. An 'Old Corps' Whig, he was to be a Lord of the Treasury 1746–54. John to his son, Pryse Campbell, 24 March 1742. Carmarthen, Dyfed Record Office, Cawdor Muniments, Box 138.

> Mr. Pulteney in his speech declared that for his own part he could have wished that the person being removed from power, might be allowed to retire in peace, but said the enquiry was necessary to satisfy the people; that is, he must sacrifice his principles, his inclinations and his good faith to popular clamour, a devil of his own raising . . . He strongly professed himself a Whig, and desired to unite us all, in the cause of liberty, and support of the present royal family; but surely it is a new way of uniting the friends of liberty, for some of them to join with the Tories, in calling the rest, and major part [of the Whigs], mercenary rascals; for if Lord Orford's [Walpole] administration was so iniquitous, what must we be, who supported and approved it. You see into what difficulties, and contradictions a man is

brought by his passions, and ambition; and affecting popularity, that is in other words, preferring the false flattery and giddy, noisy applause of knaves and fools, to the sober and sincere approbation of men of sense, and virtue, and of his own conscience.

Document 4

On the need for strong control of the Highlands, Lieutenant-General William Keppel, 2nd Earl of Albemarle, Commander-in-Chief in Scotland, to Thomas, 1st Duke of Newcastle, Secretary of State for the Southern Department. C. S. Terry ed., *Albemarle Papers* (Aberdeen, 1902) i. 289–90, 15 October 1746.

Fort George, Fort Augustus and Fort William should be made strong, defensible, and capable of containing considerable garrisons; the barrack of Inversnaid at the head of Loch Lomond should be made defensible . . . It would be highly requisite that the officers quartered in those forts and barracks proposed to be erected should be empowered to put the laws in execution that relate to the disarming of the Highlands, the change of their habit, etc. . . .

Document 5

Faced with an apparently rising tide of radical agitation, George, Marquess Townshend, Lord Lieutenant of Norfolk, wrote on 11 November 1792 to John Blofield. Oxford, Bodleian Library, Ms. Eng. Lett. c. 144 fo. 274.

The method I took on a late occasion and shall endeavour to apply again on any similar, was to summon immediately the high constables and others, and to collect tenants and neighbours to suppress any tumults and riots, to read first the Proclamation [against Seditious Meetings and Writings] and warn them of the consequence of persevering. I armed my tenants and attendants; 3 or 4 especially about me with short swords in case of any personal assault.

Document 6

The value of religious polemic in the bitterly contested 1754 Oxfordshire campaign. On 19 January 1754 *Jackson's Oxford Journal* carried an article by Thomas Bray, a Whig Fellow of Exeter College, Oxford, accusing the Tories, their ideological centre, the University of Oxford, and its Chancellor, George, 3rd Earl of Lichfield, of popery. This was in response to Tory attacks on Whig support for the Jewish Naturalisation Act. Lichfield was indeed a former Jacobite. Bray was eventually rewarded by becoming Dean of Raphoe and a canon of Christ Church. Earl Harcourt, a prominent Whig, to Bray, 22 January 1754, Exeter College Oxford, Bray papers. There are books on *The Oxfordshire Election of 1754* by R. J. Robson (Oxford, 1949) and G. H. Dannatt (Oxford, 1970).

> The charge of popery is a home thrust, and as fair a weapon in our hands, as the clamour raised against the Jews was in theirs. It has already done us infinite service, and will be a lasting advantage to us: In short there is a great deal of truth in it; and therefore is the more powerful.

Document 7

'To the Worthy Freemen of the City of York', a Whig broadsheet published in York during the general election campaign of 1747 shows the kind of argument used by the ministerial candidates. Leeds, Archives Office, Newby Hall manuscripts 2506. Associates the opposition candidates with the Jacobite threat of the '45.

> Your present, brave and disinterested behaviour gives every Englishman and Protestant exceeding pleasure: You are doing infinite honour to your city, and acting agreeably to the gallant spirit you exerted in the memorable winter in 1745. You felt your danger then . . . you knew better than I, what sort of men amongst you were ready to call in the enemy to plunder and burn your City . . . That danger in particular is past, but those who concurred to bring it on us are alive and active. You know and converse with some of them every day of your lives . . . are you for King George, or the Pretender? For Popery or the Church of England? For Peace and Law, or Rebellion and Mischief? For King

George, or King Lewis [Louis XV] of France? For the Pretender is a Puppet, and a Tool of the Pope . . . these same Tories of ours are always on the same side with the French and Papists. . . .

Document 8

Electoral interest and independence. The 1768 election at Preston was one of the bitterest contests of the period. The borough had for long been controlled by the corporation and the neighbouring gentry and there had been no contest since 1741. In 1768 the corporation candidates, local gentry, were challenged by Sir Henry Hoghton, a Dissenter, and Colonel John Burgoyne, brother-in-law of Lord Strange, the heir to the Earl of Derby, who had a considerable estate in Preston. Miners from Derby's collieries terrorised the town and Burgoyne went to the poll with a military escort and a loaded pistol in each hand. In 1661 the House of Commons had determined that the right of election was in the inhabitants, which had been understood to mean the resident freemen. The contest led to two polls, the first, of freemen alone, leading to a victory for the corporation candidates, the second, of the inhabitants, producing a contrary result. Government backing led to the vindication of the Burgoyne/Hoghton return. The contest produced much literature in an attempt to persuade an electorate of over five hundred freemen, or over eight hundred inhabitants, including the following flysheet in favour of the corporation candidates. Preston, Lancashire Record Office, DDPr 131/7.

To the worthy and independent Freemen of the Borough of Preston in the Interest of the Baronets.

The noble Effort you again make in the cause of Liberty, is the admiration of, and endears you to ev'ry honest Briton: The Infamous attempt now made to Subvert the constitution of your Borough; deserves the contempt and Detestation, with which you treat it, and the Event, I make no doubt, will once more Convince the Author of the faction against you, that no Lordly Tyranny or Oppression, shall ever be introduc'd here, nor shall this Borough ever be annexed to any Family, for its ever envied Independence to be trampled upon by, or Subjected to, ministerial Influence.

To have an Alien too palm'd upon you! a Person without

Kindred, Connection, or Property – Disdain my Friends the thoughts – Enumerate but the generality of his Supporters? Boys false to their Engagements – Turn-coats – Persons without either Vote or Interest, the ridiculous Title of Captain conferred on 'em – Sycophants and vile Dependents – Some vain of the Ear of the Titular great – some allur'd with the expectation of Places – others with Bishoprics . . . The wages of Corruption – worthy and independent Electors indeed.

Reflect one moment of your Candidate – his being your Towns-man – his Family – Fortune – Connections – Education – Abilities and Activity – the Gentlemen of Rank, Family, Fortune and Character, not only in the Town, but thro' out the County, and the respectable Body of Tradesmen of the Borough, who support his Cause.

Weigh also the conduct of both Parties – who first introduc'd Mobs and Riots – the attempt upon Sir Frank's Life may remind you – made by a wretched set of Miscreants, – hired by such others, at half a Crown a Piece which was never yet – paid 'em – what a generous notice was taken of that outrage? and how generously since return'd? – by Swords, Shot, Bullets; and a Ream of Warrants – the mean Refuge of the weak and desperate.

A FRIEND.

Document 9

The proposals of Sir Robert Walpole's ministry for an extension of the Excise led to a political storm in early 1733. A London correspondent of Edward Hopkins, a retired MP, pointed out that the controversy might affect the forthcoming general election, due in 1734 under the Septennial Act. J. Woodricke to Hopkins, 6 February 1733, BL. Add. 64929 fo. 81.

. . . The rising tempest of an Excise which at present makes a furious roar in this town, looks as if it would not soon be calmed; for people have taken a general and violent prejudice to Sir Robert's proposal even before they know what it is; and elections being so near at hand many members will be cautious how they vote full against the bent of their electors. This makes many of opinion that Sir Robert will find this point more difficult than any he has lately attempted.

Document 10

The pressure of constituency opinion. Edward Hopkins, a former Coventry MP, writing to Sir Adolphus Oughton, a current MP, no date, dated February 1733 by the British Library, though certainly written after 14 March. BL. Add. 64929 fos 87–8.

> I am indeed persuaded that some of the subscribers have upon reading the arguments on both sides entertained a more favourable opinion of the [Excise] scheme, as several others have done, who would not send you their recantation, finding so great a number of your constituents and those of figure and great influence amongst the citizens so warmly adhering to their first notions; the force of argument has little force where [self-]interest is concerned, the ratio ultima [the ultimate goal] of traders. I am sorry that the regard you paid to what you had reason to think was the general sense of your constituents should be interpreted to your disadvantage . . . I have not been wanting in proper discourses to show how much you had neglected your own private interest in acting agreeably to the sentiments of your constituents . . .

Document 11

The Excise debates create problems for Sir Adolphus Oughton MP. Oughton to Edward Hopkins, 'Saturday the 17th', 17 March 1733 (and not 17 February as filed) BL. Add. 64929 fos 85–6. Letter also reveals difficulty of assessing local opinion in age before opinion polls.

> My colleague, yesterday lost his maidenhead [virginity] in the House, by a declaration to it, that the Coventrians had changed their opinions with regard to the Excise, which was a secret had not been revealed to me . . . makes me fancy his whole authority for such an extraordinary declaration was founded only upon 2 or 3 words in the close of a letter . . . this unexpected incident is very likely to lose me my Minorcan government, which by the way is [worth] near £2,000 per annum, and which I believe by this time I had been in possession of had not this cursed Excise affair intervened, and made the usual court artifices be put in practice upon me, of keeping it open *in terrorem* [as a warning]; however whilst I lay well intrenched behind the instructions of my constituents and kept myself in a state of neutrality I was

pretty sure, by the assistance of my friends, to have weathered the point; but this behaviour of my worthy coadjutor [colleague] having beat me out of that fastness, that behaviour, which before was in my behalf softened, with the terms of prudence and circumspection, is now deemed, the result of obstinacy and perverseness.

Document 12

Electioneering costs. In 1722 Lord Whitworth found he had to pay about £600 for a seat at Newport, Isle of Wight. BL. Add. 37588 fo. 76.

I am sorry to find corruption prevails so generally in the nation, but since it has, honest men must make use of the same means, to be in a condition of doing good, as ill-designing people employ to do harm: It would be very small prudence to be over scrupulous on such occasions.

Document 13

Electioneering costs. Sudbury, though an open borough with an electorate of about 800 freemen, was notoriously corrupt. Horace Walpole, manuscript Commonplace Book. Farmington, Connecticut, Lewis Walpole Library.

A new Parliament being summoned in 1747 Mr. Nugent carried Mr. Rigby to the Prince [of Wales] who promised to assist him with £1,000 if he would go down and stand for Sudbury in his Interest which he did, and though so populous a Town, and in which he did not know one man, he carried his Election.

Document 14

The cost of an eighteenth-century election. The constituency of Weymouth and Melcombe Regis, which returned four MPs, was controlled by three interests: the government, through the customs and the Crown quarries at Portland; a Weymouth family, the Tuckers; and George Bubb Dodington who had a country seat nearby. The agreement reached between these interests in 1744 ensured uncontested elections for over half a century, but the electors, in this case the freeholders, a body of about three hundred, still expected the customary electoral treats. Anonymous note addressed to John Tucker MP, giving costs of the four candidates. Bod. Ms. Don b 20 fo. 5. R. T. was probably his brother Richard, for many years the Mayor.

> To sundry charges paid by R. T. on the election . . . in March 1761.

To ten public house bills	£ 295 12
To thirteen other keepers where no entertainments were ordered	18 18
To the Sheriff, his Bailiff, the Town Clerk and his assistant	69 6
To the Chairmen, Sergeants, Constables and Musicians	37 16

In 1762 one of the successful candidates, Sir Francis Dashwood, was appointed Chancellor of the Exchequer and, having thus accepted a place, had to seek re-election. Though unopposed, he had to spend £285 12s, including £201 19s 6d for entertainments (fo. 11).

Document 15

The nature of politics in a constituency with a small electorate is revealed in a letter sent by Thomas Orby Hunter, MP for Winchelsea and an office holder in the government, to Henry Pelham, First Lord of the Treasury. Sent on 28 March 1747, as preparations were being made for a general election, the letter concerned the most influential local politician, Edwin Wardroper. Pelham's direct interest is clear. He wished to ensure the defeat of Winchelsea's other MP, Viscount Doneraile, a critic of the government. In Winchelsea the right of election was held by resident freemen paying scot and lot. New Haven, Beinecke Library, Osborn Shelves, Pelham Box.

> When I had the honour to take my leave of you, you ordered me to send you a list of the freemen of Winchelsea . . . It is my opinion that nothing can be done without Wardroper, for he has an undoubted command over a majority of the freemen of the place and keeps the mayoralty between Parnell his brother in law, and himself.

List of Freemen of Winchelsea

1. Martin – supervisor of the Riding Officers – Wardroper's friend.

2. Parnell – Present mayor, and returning officer – Wardroper's brother in law.

3. Catt – Lord Donraile's tenant – Attached to Wardroper.

4. Old Knight – Lord Donraile's tenant – Attached to Wardroper.

5. Pavis – has a superannuation – Attached to Wardroper.

6. Voulden – lately made riding officer – Attached to Wardroper.

7. Brown – formerly servant to Martin – Attached to Wardroper.

8. - Freeman lately made by Wardroper.

9. Wardroper.

The above is Wardroper's Interest of whom Martin is the only one easily to be got off.

10. Gyles – Riding Officer – no attachment.

11. Jenkins – Riding Officer $\Big\}$ Brothers jealous of Wardroper
12. Jenkins – Riding Officer

13. J. Knight – Riding Officer $\Big\}$ Their nephews
14. T. Knight – Riding Officer

15. Lord Donraile.

16. Mr. Hunter.

N. B. Wardroper can make what number of Freemen he pleases.

Document 16

The opportunism of a corrupt political world was widely taken for granted. The *World*, a leading London daily newspaper, 6 March 1792.

> So long ago as the days of Sir Robert Walpole, the scarcity of *Patriotism* was a ground of complaint. Sir Robert used to say, he could produce patriotism when he pleased . . . By refusing an unreasonable demand, you shall next day see a man start up a violent Patriot.

Document 17

Far from having any sense that the Old Corps were in secure control of the system, the Duke of Newcastle urged the uncertainty of events as a reason for calling an election at a fortunate conjuncture in 1747, a year before it was necessary under the Septennial Act. Newcastle to Cumberland, 17 March 1747. Windsor Castle, Royal Archives, Cumberland papers 20/415.

> any final conclusion of the war, by almost any peace that can be obtained; would undoubtedly give strength to opposition, raise some flame in the nation, and render the choice of a Parliament more difficult . . . The present *New Opposition* is yet unsupported, unconnected, and not in high reputation; what the course of a year may produce nobody can tell; unfortunate public events, or private disappointments and personal views may render that opposition formidable, which at present is far from being so.

Document 18

Policies keeping governments in power. Henry Fox, MP 1735–63, ministerial officeholder 1737–56, 1757–65, discussing Walpole, his former patron, 2 December 1755. W. Cobbett, *Parliamentary History of England* xv, 597.

> To talk of a venal majority at his beck, in Parliament, may teach the people without doors to think at least, if not to talk, of a venal majority in our present Parliament. That minister, it is true, had a very great influence for many years in Parliament, but it proceeded from the rectitude of his measures, and his abilities in explaining them to the House. He was always for keeping his Countrymen in peace, if possible.

Document 19

The role of political interests. Viscount Hampden writing about his son's parliamentary candidature to George Grenville, former 'Prime Minister', 2 August 1767. Huntington Library, Stowe papers, STG. Box 22 (38).

> I have ventured to lay hold of the favourable disposition of the chief inhabitants of Lewes, backed up by the Bishop of Durham's, and the Duke of Newcastle's interest there, to set him up,

as a candidate for that borough; and at present I have no appre-
hension of any competitor.

Document 20

Local political feeling and ducal electioneering. In fact, though
the county seats and the representation of seven of the county's
boroughs were uncontested, there were contests in Bramber and
Lewes. Viscount Hampden to George Grenville, 24 August 1767,
Huntington Library, Stowe papers, STG. Box 22 (39).

> My son has not met with a single negative in his canvass: a few
> of the gentlemen of the place grumble a little at the Duke's going
> as far from home as Hertfordshire, to pick out a colleague for
> him; but no competitor has yet been, nor I hope, will be started.
> The old Duke did the honours of the county and town surpris-
> ingly; and has great reason to be pleased with the unanimous
> respect shown him by all his countrymen: – I don't foresee, at
> present, a single contest in the whole county of Sussex.

Document 21

Political issues and electoral interest: seeking support for the
Tory George Fox in the Yorkshire by-election. The recipient's
son, John, Viscount Perceval, an opposition Whig, was then
standing in alliance with the Tory, Charles Edwin, for election as
MP for Westminster, and had married in 1737 Lady Catherine
Cecil, sister of James, Earl of Salisbury, a Yorkshire landowner.
In seeking to enlist the support of the Cecil interest, Mrs Fox
mentions Turner's 'former actions', presumably his support of
Walpole. The letter can be seen as a Tory attempt to win opposition Whig support. Harriet Fox, wife of George Fox, to Catherine, Countess of Egmont, 10 October 1741. BL. Add. 47000 fo.
116.

> As Mr. Fox has the honour to be nominated a candidate for this
> county in the room of the late Lord Morpeth, I think myself
> obliged to omit no means that can be of service to him at the
> ensuing election, which is the occasion of the freedom I take in
> sending your Ladyship a few lines on public affairs; but now to
> explain my preface – Lord Salisbury has a considerable estate
> and interest in Yorkshire, Mr. Fox wrote to him soon after the

meeting of the gentlemen at York, to beg his approbation and concurrence with their nomination, but having received no answer yet from my Lord, believe the Post House has been unjust to Mr. Fox by delay of the letter, for as my Lord has always espoused the true interest of his country I flatter myself his declaration will be in Mr. Fox's favour [section missing, ending possibly 'to judge'] by his former actions, of Placemen and Pensioners . . . my Lord's speedy influence to his tenants whom to vote for, will be of infinite service to Mr. Fox to have the knowledge off, in this warm contest he is now engaged in, and as I am well assured you are always ready to serve your friends, shall believe your Ladyship's solicitations as you have so near an alliance to his family will be the most effectual means to procure my Lord's determinations.

Document 22

Tending a constituency was not just a matter of patronage. It was also necessary to ensure a favourable political atmosphere. John Tucker, MP for Weymouth, wrote to his brother Richard, his agent there, 16 December 1742. Bod. Don. c. 105 fos 200–1.

I hope Mr. Mayor and all our friends are sensible I have neglected nothing in my power for the Cause and if I have earned their friendship and good will it will be some relief . . . You'll communicate this letter to Mr. Mayor as you do all our correspondence of this sort I hope and you will speak of it to the Club in such a manner as he may think advisable.

Document 23

Speech of Humphry Sturt, MP for Dorset 1754–84, at a 1761 election meeting. Bod. MS. Don. 20 b. 20.

Then Mr. Sturt in seeming confusion said something of his having had the honour too of representing the county for which he esteemed himself greatly obliged and honoured. That he hoped he had done his duty, and if he should have the honour of serving them again that he intended something which I could not hear or distinguish, but there was the word Independency uttered and by that time he seemed to be at a loss, and so in short made a very humble bow, as if he would implore the company's understanding that he meant something very handsome and obliging and so sat down.

Document 24

Political debate in the provinces. Account of Dorchester meeting to pass an Address of Thanks to William Pitt for his conduct in the Regency Crisis. Henry Bankes, MP for Corfe Castle, government supporter, George Damer, MP for Dorchester and Charles Sturt, MP for Dorset, opposition supporters. *Salisbury and Winchester Journal,* 2 February 1789.

> Mr. Banks spoke for an hour and a half paying the highest compliments to the administration of Mr. Pitt and entered at large into the vindication of his (Mr. Banks's) parliamentary conduct, arising from an attack made on him by Mr. Damer . . . Mr. Sturt, in an animated speech of considerable length, objected to the Address, as being totally unnecessary, and tending to create animosities and discontents through the country . . . As an independent gentleman . . . He entered at large into many unpopular acts of Mr. Pitt, particularly his Commutation and Fortification Bills, and made his objections to the Address with that manly and independent spirit, as reflects the highest credit on his public character.

Document 25

The excellence of the British constitution, comparable to motion of natural bodies and reflected in use of mechanical language. Address to the public. *The Senator: or, Parliamentary Chronicle,* I (1791) iii. The appearance of this periodical testified to public interest in Parliament.

> . . . that firmness, beauty, and magnificence of our excellent Constitution, founded on the mutual consent of Prince and People; both moving, as it were, in one orb, reciprocally influencing, attracting, and directing each other; whose united power may be compared to a machine for the determining the equality of weights; the Sovereign, and the representative Body, counterpoising each other, and the Peers preserving the equilibrium.

Document 26

Unpopular government measure, the Jewish Naturalisation Act, affects election campaign. Nathaniel Cole to James Brockman, 11 September 1753. BL. Add. 42591 fo. 146. Sir Edward was the Tory candidate for Kent, Sir Edward Dering, MP there since 1733.

. . . the Jew Bill which makes so much noise everywhere has he thinks got Sir Edward at least 500 votes. The clamour this bill has occasioned is really surprising and general.

On 29 September Cole wrote again predicting accurately the repeal of the Act (fo. 148). The repeal was to help the Whig government win the 1754 election. Dering was defeated.

. . . for whether the law is right or wrong the Bill is so unpopular that I imagine no Gentleman will hazard his election by opposing such a motion.

Document 27

Attack on Pitt's populism. Extract from draft of an unpublished pamphlet by John, 2nd Earl of Egmont (1711–70) MP. (Irish and most Scottish peers, as well as those holding English courtesy titles were not members of the Westminster House of Lords and could therefore be MPs.) James Harrington's *Commonwealth of Oceana* was published in 1656. The 'two Lords' are the Duke of Newcastle and his ally Philip, 1st Earl of Hardwicke. BL. Add. 47012 B.

The defect of this mixed form of Government could never escape the notice of a man, who had raised himself from nothing, by availing himself of that defect in similar conjunctures. Harrington with great penetration and strong sense was the first who discovered, or at least the first who dared proclaim the weakness of a constitution in theory so fine, compounded of 3 parts supposed of equal authority but of distinct rights and designed to have different interests, that from interest as well as duty they might control each other, nothing but confusion has arisen from it. In times of peace and public prosperity at home the King and the Lords are too hard for the democratical part of the constitution and too often abuse it. In times of war and public calamity the popular scale preponderates in a degree which tends to a dissolution of Government, the more dangerous as its effects tend to the destruction of all order, as its motions are rapid to its end, as it never was nor ever can be guided with judgment or from becoming the dupe of the desperate and bad men who flatter it till they can have no occasion to use it . . . Pitt knew this defect in the constitution of this country, but he knew for he had tried and used, other fatal defects in the character of the people. The change of the Royal Family at the Revolution [1688, and] the convulsions before the Revolution, had formed violent parties unknown to other states. Besides the spirit of contention therefore in the different orders of the state, there was a spirit of hatred in a party to the Family upon the Throne.

What was singular in Pitt was that he alone of all the leaders in opposition had found the way to set fire to all these combustibles at once . . . hated by the superior orders of the kingdom, and condemned by the most knowing and desperate therefore of a reconciliation or of acquiring a lead of them, even a kind of necessity obliged him, if his natural genius had not inclined him, to form his system of politics, and to found his projects as he did.

Enough has been said to discover why he has ever been so inconsiderable in times of quiet, and his being so important in times of public distress. Those times were now come through the weakness and want of foresight and selfish disposition of the two Lords, whose politics centred wholly in retaining themselves in power in the House of Peers from sessions to sessions by dividing, advancing and letting down and knocking the heads together of the only significant men in the House of Commons.

Document 28

Public political dissension did not cease when Britain went to war, as Sir Robert Walpole discovered when the War of Jenkins's Ear broke out in 1739. He succeeded, however, in retaining control of Parliament, and his ally, the Duke of Newcastle, mistakenly thought that the general election of 1741 would go well. In his letter of 16 March 1741 to his nephew, Henry, 9th Earl of Lincoln, as in so much correspondence of the period, there is a lack of clarity over the political opinion that counted and a failure to predict accurately. The energy devoted to drawing up lists of voter intentions and parliamentary affiliations reflected not only the need and wish to assess strength, but also the very independence and volatility of people at different levels in the political system. BL. Add. 33065 fo. 397.

> Notwithstanding everything has been done that could possibly be thought on, to carry on this necessary war against the Spaniards, with vigour and success, the spirit of opposition will never be at rest; and great industry has been used to make the world believe that the war was either ignorantly, or knavishly carried on; But that has not prevailed; and I think, people are so convinced of the contrary, that this session, which has hitherto been the most successful of any we have of late had, will certainly end so; and there is no doubt, but we shall have a new Parliament, as good as this.

Document 29

Restrictions on parliamentary reporting. Far from being a political culture in which the discussion and formulation of policy were public, there were persistent attempts to limit available information. Resolution, 28 February 1729, *Journals of the House of Commons*, XXI, p. 238.

> That it is an indignity to and a breach of the privilege of this House for any person to presume to give, in written or printed newspapers, an account or minutes of the debates or other proceedings of this House, or any Committee thereof. That upon discovery of the authors, printers or publishers of any such written or printed newspaper, this House will proceed against the offenders with the utmost severity.

Document 30

Sir Robert Walpole complains about the partisan nature of parliamentary reporting, 13 Ap. 1738. Cobbett x. 809.

> I have read some debates of this House in which I have been made to speak the very reverse of what I meant. I have read others of them wherein all the wit, learning, and the argument has been thrown into one side, and on the other nothing but what was low, mean, and ridiculous.

Document 31

Political uncertainty at the time of Walpole's fall. Edward Southwell, opposition Whig MP, to a constituent, Michael Becher, 12 February 1742. Bristol, Public Library, Southwell papers vol. 7.

till the changes in the Ministry are settled nothing else foreign or domestic will be thought of . . . Who can tell whether a new ministry will send new armaments and reinforcements and raise such vast supplies as a vigorous general war may require or whether they will plead the bad measures and ruinous situation which their predecessors left affairs in as an argument for peace disadvantageous in itself but what they are not the cause and authors of . . . ?

Document 32

Political tension was far from constant. Alongside the habitual scholarly stress on crisis, it is important to note very different situations. Charles Wyndham MP, later 2nd Earl of Egremont, to his grand-uncle, the 6th Duke of Somerset, 28 March 1748. Exeter, Devon CRO., 1392 M/L18 48/1.

It is now very near three months since I left London, little thinking I should stay so long out of it: my first design was to stay here three weeks, except anything extraordinary happened in Parliament, in which case I desired my friends to summon me, determined to obey the summons at a day's warning: but instead of anything happening there, almost every letter I have had, has been to tell me, that the house was ill attended, and nothing likely to come on worth attending.

Document 33

Though the Bute ministry's policy of peace was generally supported, Earl Granville (formerly John, Lord Carteret), Lord President of the Council, emphasised the patronage resources at the government's disposal. Charles, 2nd Earl of Egremont, Secretary of State, reporting Granville's views, to Bute, 11 October 1762. Mount Stuart, Cardiff Mss 7/170.

. . . had no doubt of carrying the affairs of Parliament through as well as the King could wish: if the powers of the government

147

(which he lamented not having been sooner exerted) were now put in their full force. But he desired me to say very plainly, that the measure being once taken to discipline the Parliament troops, any relaxation afterwards would be decisively fatal: that no rank nor title must protect a man from instant resentment who would not concur with the measures of government, and that upon that tenure only persons must hold the great offices of the state, or aspire to the graces of the Crown: this steadily pursued he answered for success; this departed from, he saw success impossible: and that this might be the more easily be held forth by our master, as the common support of the measures was all he wanted; no particular exceptionable jobs either at home or abroad, wanted to be swallowed by the Parliament.

Document 34

1783: a sense of political malaise.

(*a*) John, 2nd Earl of Buckinghamshire, a former diplomat, took time off from admiring the scantily-clad bathing beauties at Weymouth to meditate on the crisis. Buckinghamshire to Sir Charles Hotham, 12 July 1783. Hull, University Library DDHo/4/22.

this unhappily disgraced country surrounded by every species of embarrassment, and without even a distant prospect of establishing an Administration so firm and so respectable as to restore to England any proportion of her defeated dignity. The state is now circumstanced as a human body in the last stage of a decline. Whig as I am and sufficiently vain of my descent from Maynard and Hampden, it sometimes occurs to me that something might be obtained by strengthening the hands of the Crown.

(*b*) Reverend Thomas Brand to Reverend Robert Wharton, 16 April 1783. Durham, University Library, Wharton papers. The deletion is in the original.

... the history of Party for so I think the history of modern Great Britain should be called. It is really a dreadful thing. If the King had any sinister views, what an opportunity to increase his prerogative for surely the nation must be sick of ~~politics~~ [*sic*] Patriots.

Document 35

Role of independent MPs. *Daily Universal Register*, 15 January 1785.

> Mr. Pitt has more to dread from the opposition of the independent country gentlemen, than the most formidable avowed opposition in the House of Commons. It is the independent part of the country who feel the taxes, and these are known to the first who create party and set their faces against them.

Document 36

Wooing London. In late 1721 an alliance between the Tories and a group of dissident Whigs began a bitter parliamentary attack on the Whig government designed to discredit it before the general election due in 1722. The dining of prominent politicians with the Lord Mayor was seen as a means of maintaining party loyalty and morale. Mr Rawstone to the prominent Tory, Thomas, 3rd Earl of Strafford, 26 December 1721. BL. Add. 63469 fo. 137.

> Give me leave my lord to return you thanks for the honour of your visit and being now a little freer from pain have time to recollect what your lordship was pleased to intimate of yours and some other lords' intentions of dining with my lord mayor this week or not. You may be assured he will take it to be as great an honour as can be done him, and it will give life to the honest part of the City. It has often been practiced by another party (with too much success) in this manner to keep up the spirits and support their interest here.

Document 37

The ideology of conservatism. Edward Nares, a well-connected Anglian cleric, son-in-law of the Duke of Marlborough and in 1813–41 Regius Professor of Modern History at Oxford, contrasts the historical perspective with the destructive secular philosophy of present-mindedness. Nares came to the reassuring conclusion that British victories proved divine support.

A Sermon Preached at the Parish Church of Shobdon . . . December 19, 1797 [1798]

. . . in the course of human events, a direction marvellously conducive to the final purposes of Heaven, the constant and eternal will of God; and continually illustrative of his irresistible supremacy, his over-ruling providence, his might, majesty, and power! . . . the enemy begin their operations on the pretended principle of giving perfect freedom to the mind of man. I call it a pretended principle, not only because their subsequent actions have been entirely in contradiction to it, but because, in fact no principle, as the world at present stands, could be found more inimical to the real interests of human nature. For it is plain, that the first step to be taken in vindication of such a principle, is to discard all ancient opinions as prejudices; every form of government, however matured by age, is to be submitted afresh to the judgement and choice of the passing generation, and the Almighty to be worshipped (if at all) not according to the light vouchsafed to our forefathers, but as every short-lived inhabitant of the earth shall, in his wisdom, think proper and sufficient.

Document 38

Role of press in election reporting. Report in the *Caledonian Mercury* about William Pulteney's defeat of Sir John Gordon for Cromarty in 1768, leads Pulteney to reply. Each man had gained six votes, the election meeting had split up into two parties, each of which elected its own candidate, and the sheriff had returned Pulteney. Press report seen as crucial to shaping national response to local events. James Crawford to William Pulteney, 11 May 1768. Huntington Library, Pulteney Mss, 121.

I see your letter in answer to Sir John's has been published. – It was proper on many accounts to do so – 1st To stop the mouths of the public who were making a great clamour 2ndly The Court of Session who may have taken an early prejudice which would not have been easily overcome and lastly the House of Commons, some of whom on seeing Sir John's side without an answer, might have engaged for him as believing all that he said to be true. No reply has as yet been published here nor do I think any will – If any is published, the publishers should be called to account if that can be done.

Document 39

Concern about praise for French developments: a contributor to the *Leeds Intelligencer* of 2 March 1790 attacks the idea of repealing the Test Act.

> Since last year, a reinforcement of reasons *for laying all things open* has been imported from France, and we are reproached with falling so far short of the liberality of sentiment displayed in that Kingdom. I love liberty as well as any man, but not that particular species of it, which allows only seven minutes to prepare for death, before one is hanged up by fish-women at a lampiron; and though superstition be a very bad thing, I hope never to see the British National Assembly possessed by the spirit of Voltaire.

Document 40

Tory hostility to the 'moneyed interest' and the allegedly corrupting power of wealth can be seen in Jonathan Swift's *The Conduct of the Allies* (1711), Swift, *Prose Works* vi, 10.

> a Set of Upstarts, who had little or no part in the *Revolution*, but valued themselves by their Noise and pretended Zeal when the Work was over, were got into Credit at Court, by the Merit of becoming Undertakers and Projectors of Loans and Funds: These, finding that the Gentlemen of Estates were not willing to come into their Measures, fell upon those new Schemes of raising Money, in order to create a Mony'd Interest, that might in time vie with the Landed, and of which they hoped to be at the Head.

Document 41

The pessimistic Tory realisation of the fallibility of human ambitions and schemes as opposed to the optimistic Whig assessment of the possibility of establishing consistent policies and creating a predictable and stable order. Dr Samuel Johnson, *Thoughts on the late Transactions respecting Falkland's Islands* (1771), pp. 33–4.

> It seems to be almost the universal error of historians to suppose it politically, as it is physically true, that every effect has a proportionate cause. In the inanimate action of matter upon matter, the motion produced can be but equal to the force of the moving power; but the operations of life, whether private or

public, admit no such laws. The caprices of voluntary agents laugh at calculation . . . Obstinacy and flexibility, malignity and kindness, given place alternately to each other, and the reason of these vicissitudes . . . often escapes the mind in which the change is made.

Document 42

Edmund Burke was for long dissatisfied with the attitude of the Pitt government towards Revolutionary France and British radicals. Burke to James, 1st Lord Malmesbury, 10 September [1792]. Winchester, Hampshire CRO. Malmesbury papers vol. 145.

> The English assassins of the Jacobin faction are working hard to corrupt the public mind in favour of their brother murderers in France – and not *one* person, either on the part of government, or opposition makes the slightest effort, of any kind, to prevent the ill effects of these poisons. I am, I confess, sick at heart from all these horrors and perfectly disgusted with the conduct or rather no conduct of both parties, at a time when neutrality does not nor cannot produce neutral effects.

Document 43

The upsurge of radicalism in response to the French Revolution leads to conservative calls for a programme of indoctrination in order to achieve an acceptable politicisation of the country. William, Lord Auckland MP, Ambassador to the United Provinces, to William, Lord Grenville, Foreign Secretary, 26 November 1792. BL. Add. 58920 fos 178–9.

> . . . every possible form of Proclamations to the People, orders for Fast Days, Speeches from the Throne, Discourses from the Pulpit, Discussions in Parliament etc. I am sure that we should gain ground by this. The prosperity and opulence of England are such, that except the lowest and most destitute class, and men of undone fortunes and desperate pursuits, there are none who would not suffer essentially in their fortunes, occupations, comfort, in the glory, strength and well-being of their country, but above all in that sense of security which forms the sole happiness of life, by this new species of French disease which is spreading its contagion among us . . . the abandoning of religion is a certain step towards anarchy.

Document 44

Radicalism v. Loyalism.

(*a*) John Hatsell, Clerk to the House of Commons, to John Ley, 28 November 1792. Exeter, Devon CRO. 63/2/11/1/53.

I wish every county was like Devonshire – but I fear, that in Ireland, Scotland, the manufacturing parts of Yorkshire and particularly in London, there is a very different spirit rising . . . the Society at the Crown and Anchor. This appears to me a better plan than trusting to the soldiery and brings the question to its true point – a contest between those who have property and those who have none – If this idea is followed up generally and with spirit, it may, for a time, secure us peace *internally*.

(*b*) Duke of Portland, leader of the opposition in the House of Lords, to William Windham MP, a Whig who followed Burke in his hostility to the French Revolution. As a result of the Revolution. Portland and Windham were to come to support Pitt, 13 October 1792. BL. Add. 37845 fo. 5. Portland was confident:

there is too large a portion of good sense, or self interest, or indolence, or indecision, or dislike of novelty or attachment to old habits, or in short something that if it is not good sense, will be a substitute for it which will prevent our being overrun by French principles.

Document 45

In an apparently revolutionary crisis, it was essential to create an impression of strength. Asserting Lancastrian loyalty, *Wheeler's Manchester Chronicle* of 22 December 1792 published accounts of loyalist anti-Painite demonstrations, attacked Paine and denied radical claims.

It is extraordinary with what industry blazoned accounts have been sent to the London papers, of riots that never existed in this town . . . the bent of the people is peaceable, with a satisfied continuance at those employments which their various duties call them to . . . the People, all over the kingdom, have spontaneously made the principles of the present constitution, the standard of their affection, with a determined resolution to reject wild theories, and support that kind of Government, which is so happily calculated to protect their persons and property in return.

Document 46

The need for major change in Ireland was very much stressed in the quarter-century before the Union. William, 1st Marquess of Lansdowne, formerly, as 2nd Earl of Shelburne, first minister and major Irish landowner, to Silver Oliver MP, 26 July 1786. Bowood, Shelburne papers, Box 59. In light of Catholic agitation and terrorism, the anti-tithe Rightboy movement, Lansdowne urges a change in the position of the established (Anglican) Church. On the movement, see J. S. Donnolly, 'The Rightboy movement', *Studia Hibernica*, XVII–XVIII (1977–8), pp. 120–202; M. J. Bric, 'Priests, parsons and politics: the Rightboy protest in County Cork, 1785–1788', *Past and Present*, C (1983), pp. 100–23.

It appears to me morally impossible, that in times like the present, two million and a half of people can long continue to pay so burthensome a tax as that of tithe to the Clergy of only two or three hundred thousand, be they ever so respectable . . . I earnestly wish that the Bishops and the Clergy would take the lead upon the present occasion; first, by rectifying such abuses as are universally acknowledged . . . particularly those of Pluralities and non residence . . . As to tithe, it is inconceivable to me, what objection the Clergy can possibly have to commute them for Land, as the advantages appear . . . manifold . . . They would become by means of it immediately a part of Society, instead of a burden upon it, and consequently be no longer liable to be struck off by any political convulsion – They would enjoy a real and original power, by possessing the two great sources of it, Property and Residence, in addition to their Patronage, and the great influence which must arise from their Functions being well administered, and their Character – They would be a support to all parts of Government and the Constitution, instead of being a weight upon both . . . Reverse the Medal . . . the times are unfavourable to the Clergy both at home and abroad . . . Foreign intrigue will necessarily, after what has lately happened in America, mix in these disturbances . . . Faction will inflame things . . . the Church of England runs the risk of falling in Ireland and if great care is not taken all Property and Government will be endangered at the same time . . . Force never has effected good on either side, and on which ever side it is exerted, carries with it something abhorrent to our manners and Government. Preventive wisdom is certainly the greatest qualification

which Government can have . . . the circumstances of Ireland
and England are so very different, in regard to Religion, that they
must necessarily require a different system in that respect.

Document 47

A sense of crisis. On 27 August 1778, John, 3rd Earl of Bristol, a
critic of the government, wrote from his splendid seat at Ickworth
to the Earl of Shelburne. Bowood, Shelburne papers, Box 36.

These accumulated Evils are really too much not to feel, and
wish to resist in an effectual manner: what is to become of us,
are we determined to submit, and be tamely sacrificed or not?
Do not the real friends of this country wish for some meetings,
in order to endeavour to stem the torrent of destruction? . . . all
the zealous wellwishers of the King and Country, must collect
and unite under one great principle of disinterested zeal.

Document 48

A sense of crisis, 1783. The new Foreign Secretary, Francis, Mar-
quis of Carmarthen, explaining why he had taken office: to help
protect George III and the constitution from the Fox–North ministry. Carmarthen to Shelburne, 31 December 1783. Bowood,
Shelburne papers, Box 39.

The singular I wish I was not obliged to add unfortunate situation in which the mad violence of certain persons had involved
the public, rendered it, from motives of the most disinterested
duty, incumbent upon me . . . . should we maintain our Ground,
we shall certainly have done some service in having rescued
both Crown and People, from the daring attempt, to establish a
system of corrupt influence . . . at the hazard of sacrificing the
constitution.

Document 49

The Political Crisis of early 1784. Ministry of Pitt the Younger
supported by George III and the majority in the House of Lords,
but lacks majority in Commons. George III to General Richard
Grenville, Comptroller of the household of Frederick, Duke of
York, 13 February 1784. BL. Add. 70957.

the present strange phenomenon, a majority not exceeding 30 in the House of Commons thinking that justifies the stopping the necessary supplies when the House of Lords by a majority of near two to one and at least that of the People at large approve of my conduct and see as I do that not less is meant than to render the Crown and the Lords perfect cyphers; but it will be seen that I will never submit to so degrading a situation.

Document 50

The reversionary interest. In November 1759 Henry Legge, the Chancellor of the Exchequer, stood for Hampshire supported by the most influential local aristocrat, the Duke of Bolton, and by the Duke of Newcastle, then First Lord of the Treasury. He was opposed by Simeon Stuart who was supported by those opposed to the Bolton interest, especially James, Marquess of Carnarvon, MP for Winchester and the heir to the other leading Hampshire magnate, the Duke of Chandos. Carnarvon secured the backing of Prince George, the future George III, but Legge's superiority led Stuart to back down without a struggle. Legge was then pressed by George's adviser, the Earl of Bute, to promise support in the next general election. Legge's refusal angered George, who dismissed him in March 1761. Lord Bute's answer, no date but late 1759. Manchester, John Rylands Library, Eng. Mss. 668 15.

The instant Mr. Legge represents Himself as Bound in Honour not to decline standing for Hampshire at the next general Election, Lord Bute is firmly persuaded that the Prince will by no means desire it of Him: But he does, out of real Friendship to Mr. Legge, beseech Him to consider very seriously, whether after triumphing over the Prince's Inclinations at Present, Lord Bute hath any Method Left of removing prejudices that the late unhappy Occurrences have strongly impressed the Prince with, than by being enabled to assure Him that Mr. Legge will as far as shall be in his Power cooperate with his Royal Highness's Wishes at the next general Election.

Document 51

Assassination attempt on George III leads him to note his popularity, but also to refer to the threat of irresponsible rule posed by the reversionary interest. George to Richard Grenville, 29 August 1786. BL. Add. 70957.

> I have every reason to be satisfied with the impressions it has awakened in this country where perhaps my life is at present of more consequence than I could wish.

Document 52

Parliamentary reform divided the government in 1785. Supported by Pitt, it was opposed by George III and a host of prominent figures, such as Grenville and John, 3rd Duke of Dorset, a royal favourite and Ambassador in Paris. Dorset provided an authentic voice of conservatism. Dorset to Nathaniel Wraxall MP, 17 March 1785. New Haven, Beinecke Library, Osborn Files, Dorset.

> as to the reform I wish to god he may be beaten by a thumping majority. It is too foolish a thing to hear of. If the *rotten boroughs* are destroyed England will soon become a rotten country and it will [be] time to seek for protection and shelter elsewhere. It seems a paradox, but it is true that the fewer means we have left us of corruption, the quicker we shall become rotten and have at last no government at all.

Bibliographical essay

This essay should be read in conjunction with the notes.

The most recent works offer in their bibliographies and footnotes guides to earlier literature. For the pre-1714 period, C. Jones ed., *Britain in the First Age of Party 1680–1750* (1987). For 1714–42, J. Black ed., *Britain in the Age of Walpole* (1984), S. Baskerville ed., *Walpole in Power, 1720–1742* (Oxford, 1985), P. Langford, *A Polite and Commercial People: England 1727–1783* (Oxford, 1989), and Black, *Robert Walpole and the Nature of Politics in Early Eighteenth-Century England* (1990). For 1742–89, Black ed., *British Politics and Society from Walpole to Pitt 1742–1789* (1990), K. Perry, *British Politics and the American Revolution* (1990). For 1783–1800, H. T. Dickinson ed., *Britain and the French Revolution, 1789–1815* (1989), J. Derry, *Politics in the Age of Fox, Pitt and Liverpool* (1990). For social background, R. Porter, *English Society in the Eighteenth Century* (2nd ed., 1990) and J. Rule, *Albion's People: English Society 1714–1815* (1992). Possibly the best approach to the period is by a careful reading of sources. Collections include D. B. Horn and M. Ransome eds., *English Historical Documents, 1714–1783* (1957), A. Aspinall and E. A. Smith eds., *English Historical Documents, 1783–1832* (1959) and E. N. Williams, *The Eighteenth-Century Constitution* (Cambridge, 1960). Parliamentary debates can be found in W. Cobbett, *A Parliamentary History of England* (1806–20), and should be used in conjunction with R. R. Sedgwick, *The History of Parliament: the House of Commons, 1715–1754* (1970) and L. Namier and J. Brooke, *The History of Parliament: the House of Commons 1754–90* (1964).

Much political correspondence was printed in the nineteenth century, especially the relevant volumes of the Historical Manuscript Commission reports and W. S. Taylor and J. H. Pringle eds., *The Correspondence of William Pitt* (1838–40); Lord John Russell ed., *The Correspondence of John, Fourth Duke of Bedford* (1842–6); W. J. Smith ed., *The Grenville Papers* (1852–3); Lord Edmond Fitzmaurice ed., *The Life of William, Earl of Shelburne* (1875–6); and W. R. Anson ed., *Autobiography and Political Correspondence of . . . Third Duke of Grafton* (1898). Unlike for his predecessors, there is a mass of surviving correspondence for George III: Sir John Fortescue ed., *The Correspondence of King George the Third from 1760 to 1783* (1927) which, however, contains numerous errors; Sedgwick ed., *Letters from George III to Lord Bute, 1756–1766* (1939) and Aspinall ed., *The Later Correspondence of George III* (Cambridge, 1962).

Recent editions of political material include W. S. Lewis ed., *The Yale Edition of Horace Walpole's Correspondence* (New Haven, 1937–83); T. W. Copeland and others eds, *The Correspondence of Edmund Burke* (Cambridge, 1958–78); J. Carswell and L. A. Dralle eds., *The Political Journal of George Bubb Dodington* (Oxford, 1965); H. L. Snyder ed., *The Marlborough–Godolphin Correspondence* (Oxford, 1975); Langford and others eds, *The Writings and Speeches of Edmund Burke* (Oxford, 1981 –); T. J. McCann ed., *The Correspondence of the Dukes of Richmond and Newcastle 1724–1750* (Lewes, 1984); Brooke ed., *Horace Walpole. Memoirs of King George II* (New Haven, 1985); J. C. D. Clark ed., *The Memoirs and Speeches of James, 2nd Earl Waldegrave 1742–1763* (Cambridge, 1988) and P. Jupp ed., *The Letter-Journal of George Canning 1793–1795* (1991). Fresh light on the administration of justice is provided by R. Paley ed., *Justice in Eighteenth-Century Hackney: the justicing notebook of Henry Norris and the Hackney Petty Sessions Book* (1991). J. Kelly eds, *The Letters of Lord Chief Baron Edward Willes to the Earl of Warwick 1757–62* (Aberystwyth, 1990) offer a valuable account of Ireland. The microfilm company Research Publications has published microfilm editions of major collections including the Blenheim, Fox, Newcastle, North and Pitt papers.

The accounts of foreign travellers throw an interesting light on British society and politics. They include C. de Saussure, *A Foreign View of England in the Reign of George II* (1902); Casanova, *Memoirs* (1940); P. Kalm, *Account of a Visit to England* (New York,

1892); and F. de la Rochefoucauld, *A Frenchman in England, 1784*, translated by S. C. Roberts (Cambridge, 1933), and by N. Scarfe in *A Frenchman's Year in Suffolk, 1784* (Woodbridge, 1989).

The world of caricature is introduced in M. Duffy ed., *The English Satirical Print 1660–1832* (Cambridge, 1986) and the press in Black ed., *The English Press in the Eighteenth Century* (1987). Newspapers of the period are available in the reference divisions of many central libraries, including those of Bristol, Gateshead, Gloucester, Leeds, Newcastle, Norwich, Reading, Sheffield and York.

The writings and correspondence of prominent literary figures were often explicitly political, and are anyway a stimulating guide to the cultural context of political life. Modern editions include D. F. Bond ed., *The Spectator* (Oxford, 1965); Bond ed., *The Tatler* (Oxford, 1987); A. Ross and D. Woolley eds, *Jonathan Swift* (Oxford, 1984); J. McMinn ed., *Swift's Irish Pamphlets* (Gerrards Cross, 1991); Jonathan Swift and Thomas Sheridan, *The Intelligencer*, ed. J. Woolley (Oxford, 1992); W. B. Coley ed., *Henry Fielding. The True Patriot and related writings* (Oxford, 1987); B. A. Goldgar ed., *Henry Fielding. The Covent Garden Journal* (Oxford, 1988); Johnson, *Political Writings* ed. D. J. Greene (New Haven, 1977); Greene ed., *Samuel Johnson* (Oxford, 1984); J. Cannon ed., *The Letters of Junius* (Oxford, 1978); A. G. Hill ed., *Letters of William Wordsworth* I (Oxford, 1984). Other works worth reading include the novels of Smollett and the plays of Foote. For background, Greene, *The Politics of Samuel Johnson* (2nd ed., Athens, Georgia, 1990), Black and J. Gregory eds, *Culture, Politics and Society in Britain, 1660–1800* (Manchester, 1991).

Biographies can be an interesting way to approach political history. Important recent scholarly ones include E. Gregg, *Queen Anne* (1980); R. Hatton, *George I: Elector and King* (1978); R. Browning, *The Duke of Newcastle* (New Haven, 1975); Black, *Pitt the Elder* (Cambridge, 1992); Brooke, *George III* (1972); P. Lawson, *George Grenville* (Oxford, 1984); P. D. G. Thomas, *Lord North* (1976); J. Ehrman, *The Younger Pitt* (1969, 1983).

Good general surveys include B. W. Hill, *The Growth of Parliamentary Parties 1689–1742* (1976) and *British Parliamentary Parties, 1742–1832* (1985) and F. O'Gorman, *The Emergence of the British Two-Party System, 1760–1832* (1982). The solid ranks of monographs should be approached after consulting more general works, but it is worth noting on elections, O'Gorman, *Voters, Patrons and Parties: the unreformed electorate of Hanoverian England, 1734–1832* (Oxford, 1989); on ideology, Dickinson, *Liberty and Property: political ideology in eighteenth-century Britain* (1977), Clark, *English Society, 1688–1832: ideology, social structure and political practice during the ancien régime* (Cambridge, 1985) and J. J. Sack, *From Jacobite to Conservative: reaction and orthodoxy in Britain, c. 1760–1832* (Cambridge, 1993); on public opinion, M. Peters, *Pitt and Popularity: the patriot minister and London opinion during the Seven Years War* (Oxford, 1980); on Ireland T. Bartlett, *The Fall and Rise of the Irish Nation: the Catholic Question 1690–1830* (Dublin, 1992); S. J. Connolly, *Religion, Law, and Power: the making of Protestant Ireland, 1660–1760* (Oxford, 1992); F. G. James, *Ireland in the Empire 1688–1770* (Cambridge, Mass., 1973); E. M. Johnston, *Ireland in the Eighteenth Century* (Dublin, 1974); R. B. McDowell, *Ireland in the Age of Imperialism and Revolution 1760–1801* (Oxford, 1979) and T. W. Moody and W. E. Vaughan eds, *Eighteenth Century Ireland 1691–1800* (Oxford, 1986); on Scotland, N. T. Phillipson and R. Mitchison, *Scotland in the Age of Improvement* (1970), B. P. Lenman, *Integration, Enlightenment and Industrialization, Scotland 1746–1832* (1981) and M. Fry, *The Dundas Despotism* (Edinburgh, 1992); on nationalism, L. Colley, *Britons* (New Haven, 1992); and on radicalism, J. G. A. Pocock ed., *Three British Revolutions: 1641, 1688, 1776* (Princeton, 1980) and M. and J. Jacobs eds, *The Origins of Anglo-American Radicalism* (1984). On political culture, E. Hellmuth ed., *The Transformation of Political Culture, England and Germany in the late eighteenth century* (Oxford, 1990), and on popular action, E. P. Thompson, *Customs in Common* (1991). State development is discussed in J. Brewer, *The Sinews of Power: war, money and the English State, 1688–1783* (1989), B. M. Downing, *The Military Revolution and Political Change: origins of democracy and autocracy in early modern Europe* (Princeton, 1992) and Black, *British Foreign Policy in an Age of Revolutions 1783–93* (Cambridge, 1994).

Index